My Father's Bitter Gift

Dorothy Eaton Watts

Review and Herald® Publishing Association
Washington, DC 20039-0555
Hagerstown, MD 21740

This book was
Edited by Raymond H. Woolsey
Cover design by Bill Kirstein
Cover illustration by Mitchel Heinze
Type set: 12/13 Palatino

PRINTED IN U.S.A.

R&H Cataloging Service

Watts, Dorothy Eaton, 1937-
  My father's bitter gift.

  1. Shipowick, Archie, 1895-   I. Title.
                    B

  ISBN 0-8280-0494-3

My Father's
Bitter Gift

Contents

Archie Rebels

Archie Shipowick shoved his right hand into the pocket of his baggy brown trousers and pulled out a muddy earthworm. Scores of the creatures had come out of hiding after the warm rain. They were everywhere: on the road, in the grass, and in the mud puddles. He had picked this one up, along with a dozen others, on his way home from the one-room schoolhouse where he would finish the eighth grade in a few days.

Straightening his shoulders, Archie felt taller than the five feet five inches that he really was. His coming graduation, the fresh, earthy smell of rain, the brilliant arch of a rainbow above the greening Russian steppe, and the oozy feel of earthworms in his pocket combined to make him feel that the world was his. Czar Nicholas in his palace could have felt no greater than Archie that May afternoon in 1909.

Stuffing the worm back into his pocket, Archie ran the rest of the way home. He threw his books and slate onto the wooden bench inside the door, grabbed his fishing pole, and called to his mother, who stood, red-faced and sweaty, by the large wall oven removing crusty loaves of rye bread.

"I'm going fishing, Mamma!"

"That's a good son," Domka Shipowick said, stopping long enough to flash an approving smile at her oldest son. Tucking a long strand of dark brown hair into the bun at the back of her neck, she said, "I'll fry them for your supper. They'll taste delicious with fresh bread, homemade cheese, and borscht."

"See that you're home before dark." His father's voice, harsh and accusing, brought Archie to a halt.

He hesitated a moment in the doorway, fishing pole in hand. His eyes narrowed into a frown and his lips tightened as he struggled to keep back the words that wanted to spill out. *What have I done now? Don't you trust me? Don't you realize that I'm almost a man? Why are you always getting after me? Why don't you talk to Mary or Roman that way? Why do Bert and Zenya get away with everything?*

Samuel Shipowick, stitching a pair of boots at his cobbler's bench, didn't notice the hostility of his teenage son. It was just as well.

Archie caught his mother's eye and knew she understood. She smiled and shook her head. Her dark eyes pled with him to be quiet. He knew she was remembering beatings his father had given him for talking back. He'd had several in the past three years.

To avoid further conflict with his father, Archie retreated into the spring sunshine. Somehow the joy had gone from his day. Even the rainbow had disappeared. Only his worms were left.

Archie kicked a stone and watched it gather mud as it rolled along the path towards the river. It came to rest in a mud puddle that was alive with wiggling earthworms. Archie picked one from the puddle's edge and ran the rest of the way to the river bank.

He placed the worm on the hook and cast his line into the swirling river. Gripping the willow pole, he straddled a fallen tree at the water's edge and waited for a bite.

"You'd think Papa would appreciate the fact I'm trying to help provide food for the family," Archie said to his fishing pole. It didn't matter that the pole couldn't answer. One of the reasons he liked coming to the river was the chance it gave him to reason things out. His life seemed to have gotten progressively worse over the past three years. Papa just didn't understand anymore.

"I do all my chores around the house," Archie thumped his pole on the log for emphasis. "I keep the yard and garden clean. I bring home fish for the family. I herd sheep to help pay the bills. I study hard at school. I can't figure it out!"

"What can't you figure out?"

Startled, Archie jerked around to see his 9-year-old brother, hands in pockets, standing on the bank. "Roman, go home where you belong!" Archie scowled.

"No!"

"Nobody asked you to come. So beat it!"

"What's eating you? You're acting like an old bear."

"You wouldn't understand. You're too young."

"You're mad at Papa, aren't you?"

"So? What else is new?"

"If you don't watch out you'll get another whipping."

"That's my business."

"Papa's been drinking and Mamma's afraid you'll make him angry again. I sure wish Papa didn't drink so much. Why does he do it?"

Archie moved on the log and motioned for his younger brother to sit down. They stared at the brown water below them for a moment. Finally, Archie spoke.

"He drinks with customers when they come to pick up the boots he's made for them." Archie paused, searching for answers for himself as well as for his brother. "I think it makes him feel important to offer vodka to his friends. He thinks that will make them come back. The only trouble is, we can't afford to buy vodka for the whole village! You need clothes and so does Mary. Mamma hasn't had a new dress in years. We need a new roof. The house needs whitewashing. We can't do anything because Papa drinks up almost all the money he makes."

"But when Papa doesn't drink he's really tops," Roman remarked.

"I know that. I just think Papa knows I don't like his drinking and that's why he gets so mad at me. One thing for sure, when I grow up I'm not going to be like Papa. I'll never drink or gamble. I'm going to make my kids happy."

"Me, too," Roman agreed.

"Come on," Archie said, pulling in his fishing line. "The fish aren't biting and I think it's time for supper. I'll beat you to the house."

Laughing and slipping in the mud, the two boys raced up the bank and across the flat grassland towards home. Their village was named Podolsk; it was in Russia, near the Romanian border. Lights were already twinkling in the small windows of the whitewashed mud brick houses. Odors of freshly baked bread and frying onions and bacon mingled with the pungent smell of smoke rising from the thatched roofed houses across the village.

"I won!" Roman laughed as he pushed open the front door and kicked off his muddy shoes.

Archie propped his fishing pole against the door jam and took a deep breath as if to brace himself for the scene he knew would come.

As quietly as he could, Archie slipped in the door and sat on the bench beside the school books he had thrown there earlier. He bent to remove his shoes, hoping his father had not noticed his arrival. Mr. Shipowick was talking loudly with a customer about the latest reforms in Moscow, and there was just a chance that Archie could take his place at the supper table without being scolded.

"Archie!" his father's voice boomed. "You're late. Didn't I tell you to come before dark?"

"Yes, sir." Archie stared defiantly at his father. He would have said more had they been alone, but Dimitri, a customer from the next village, sat on the bench next to his dad. A half empty bottle of vodka stood on the worktable beside a finished pair of brown leather boots.

Archie looked in disgust as Samuel Shipowick filled Dimitri's glass, then raised the bottle to his own lips and drained the contents.

"Best vodka in Russia!" he boasted.

"Here's to my friend Samuel, the best shoemaker there is," Dimitri raised his glass in a toast.

Grinning broadly, Archie's father jumped to his feet and grabbed the rubles lying beside the boots. "Archie, go to the liquor store and bring us a bottle of vodka. My friend and I must have another drink." He thrust the crumpled bills towards his son.

Archie sighed and looked to his mother for support, but she wasn't looking. Her back to the men, she stood at the table ladling steaming beet soup into waiting bowls. Mary, Roman, Bert, and Zenya, already seated for supper, turned to look at Archie as if expecting him to do something. Did they expect him to refuse? He couldn't do that. Not with company present. He took the money from his father's outstretched hand.

"Get moving!" his father ordered. "If you don't hurry the store will close before you get there."

Archie wheeled and went out into the night. At the

gate he turned left. He needed a few minutes to think things through. He knew he didn't want to spend the money on liquor, but he didn't know how to avoid it.

He stopped for a few minutes in the open doorway of the blacksmith shop to watch the smithy hammer red hot metal into nails. As the rhythmic hammer blows pounded the nails into shape, they seemed to straighten Archie's thinking as well.

Now was the time for him to take a stand and keep Papa from wasting his hard-earned money on liquor. Archie was, after all, the oldest boy in the family. It was up to him to do something to save the money, and now he knew what.

Archie stepped back into the night. Taking another left he walked on to the end of the row of houses. Skirting the village in a wide arc, he circled back toward home. As he passed the weather-beaten liquor store he noticed with satisfaction that it was closed.

As soon as Archie stepped inside the door at home he knew he was in for trouble. Dimitri had left with his boots. Father stood beside the workbench, hands on hips, jaw thrust forward, and chest heaving. "Archie, where in the name of all the saints have you been?"

"I went to the liquor store, Papa, but it was closed," Archie looked straight into his father's flashing blue eyes.

"You could have been there and back three times," Mr. Shipowick stormed. "I'll teach you not to pull tricks on me!"

Sixteen-year-old Mary, still seated at the supper table, covered her face to hide the pain she felt for her brother. Bert and Zenya ran to Mamma for protection. Roman sat wide-eyed, knowing what was coming.

"Please, Samuel! Spare the boy!" Mrs. Shipowick cried as she watched her husband take a long, thick leather strap from its hook on the wall.

"Stay out of this, woman!" Mr. Shipowick warned. "The boy has disobeyed and he's got to learn his lesson."

One after another the blows fell on Archie's legs and back. His thin shirt tore under the fierceness of the lash. The pain was more than he could stand. He fell onto the earthen floor at his father's feet.

In a flash Archie's mother was at his side. "Oh, Samuel, can't you stop now? You've done enough!" As she knelt over Archie to comfort him, the blows fell on her back.

His anger assuaged, Mr. Shipowick stomped out of the house, banging the door behind him.

"Mamma, are you all right?" cried Zenya, tears streaming down her cheeks.

"Why did Papa hit you?" Bert's forehead wrinkled into a puzzled frown.

"Shut up!" Roman answered. "It's because he was drunk."

"Mamma, what can I do to help?" Mary begged.

"We'll be all right." Mrs. Shipowick put an arm around Archie, helping him to stand. "I'll take Archie over to Babushka's house. You stay here and put the younger children to bed. Then clear the table and go to bed yourself."

Archie stumbled the few steps next door to his grandmother's small cottage. Two candles on the rough-hewn table cast warm shadows on the walls and lit up Babushka's wrinkled face as she sat knitting socks.

"Set yourself down and tell your old granny what happened," she said, motioning to the bench opposite her.

"Samuel beat him again," Mrs. Shipowick sighed.

"And I didn't deserve it!" Archie pounded the table,

making the candles flicker. "I was only trying to help. I hate that man! I'll never speak to him again."

"Archie!" his mother exclaimed. "Don't say that. He is your father."

"He's no father of mine."

"What foolish talk," added Grandma. "You are the spitting image of your father. You act just like he did when he was your age. You've got the same fiery spirit and . . ."

"No! No! Stop! I'm not like that man! I will never be like him. . . ." Archie's voice broke off in sobs. Running into the next room he threw himself onto the straw mattress of the smaller bed, and buried his face in the soft feather pillow.

A short while later his mother covered Archie with a patchwork comforter and returned home.

Grandma blew out the candles and shuffled to her bed beside Archie's.

"Babushka," Archie whispered into the darkness.

"Yes, Son."

"I really mean it. I'm not going back home."

"That's all right. You can stay here as long as you like. I need a man to help around the house."

With just a hint of a smile on his tear-stained face Archie turned over and snuggled deeper under the warm comforter.

Plowing Disaster

The sky was changing from violet to gold when Archie awoke the morning after his eighth grade graduation. In one swift motion he was out of bed and dressed. Towel around his neck, Grandma's homemade soap in hand, he raced out the door towards the river. A quick, cold bath would set his blood tingling, making him feel ready to tackle the world.

He wanted to look his best on this particular morning, because he, Archie Shipowick, was going to find a job. He would prove to the whole village that he was a man, able to make it on his own. Bath finished, he ran home to Babushka's cottage, threw his towel and soap on the bench, grabbed two empty water buckets, and filled them at the well. His chores done, he sat down to a bowl of steaming cornmeal mush with rich country cream.

"You eat plenty now," Grandma spooned more mush into Archie's bowl. "Today is your big day and you've got to have strength."

"Who should I try first, Babushka?" Archie asked as he spread freshly churned butter on a thick slice of rye bread.

"I'd try the landlord." Grandma squinted as she looked out the window toward the large two-storied frame house that stood like a castle on a small knoll half a mile away. Its windows, reflecting the rising sun, shone like polished brass. "You herded sheep for him last summer."

"Good idea! I'll go there now before he goes to the fields. Thanks for breakfast. See you tonight." Archie was already out the door when Grandma called after him.

"Archie, your lunch!" But he was gone.

Archie found Ivan, the rich landowner, in the granary inspecting seed-corn. He smiled as Archie approached.

"Hello, Archie. Want to herd sheep again this summer?"

"Yes, sir . . . I mean, no, sir . . . uh . . . What I mean is . . . that I've finished school and . . . uh . . . I'm on my own now . . . and . . ."

"I see," Ivan turned from inspecting corn to study the boy's earnest face. "You were looking for more of a man's job, eh? Can you handle a plow?"

"Yes, sir. I helped old Vasili plow his sugar beet field last year."

"Can you manage four horses?"

"No problem."

"Can you start today?"

"Sure thing."

"Come, then. I'll help you harness the horses, then I'll show you where to start."

Within an hour Archie was on his own, behind four horses, turning wide furrows of rich, black soil. The sun beat warm on his back. The scent of apple blossoms drifted across the field. His spirit soared with the swallows that darted above him. Like them he was free—free from school, free from his father's tirades, free from his past, and free from trouble.

Not quite. Suddenly the plow jumped out of the

ground as it came to a hard path where villagers crossed the field. On the other side Archie maneuvered the plow back into the soil but not without making a few bends in the furrow. Coming back, the same thing happened.

When Ivan returned at mid-morning he walked up and down the furrows scowling. "Archie, you can do better than this! Your furrows are as crooked as a ram's horn running down to Jericho! I want this path plowed up. Make the furrows straight. I'll be back in an hour and I expect this corrected."

"I'm sorry, sir. I'll do it over. I'll make the rows straight," Archie promised, swallowing hard.

"You'd better!" the landlord called over his shoulder.

Archie was determined to find a way to cut through the hard path. As he neared the spot on the next round he jumped onto the plow with both feet, thinking his weight would keep the plow in the ground.

It jumped again. Archie's feet slipped. The horses pulled the plow over his left foot, cutting an eight-inch gash across the sole.

"Woa! Woa!" Archie shouted. The horses stopped. He felt sick at the sight of his own red blood mingling with the black soil. Frantically he pulled off his shirt and tore it into strips, which he wound around the gaping wound.

Hearing Archie's cry, Ivan spun around and guessed what had happened. Dashing back across the field he panted, "I'll take care of the horses. You'd better go home. Can you make it alone?"

"I think so."

Fortunately it wasn't far. He hobbled as far as the door and collapsed on the bench.

"Archie! What happened?" Grandma looked up from the table where she stood rolling out dough for potato dumplings. Dusting her hands on the sides of

her large apron, she crossed the room and took Archie
by the arm. "I'll help you to bed."

"I can't go any further."

"Yes, you can. Just a few more steps. I can care for
you better in there." Half carrying him, half dragging
him, Grandma got Archie to bed. After making him
comfortable, she unwrapped the bandage, which was
now caked with dirt and dried blood. Tenderly she
washed the wound and applied a generous poultice of
her special herbal powder.

"There now. You'll be as good as new before you
know it."

"I'm . . . not . . . going . . . to lose my foot?"

"No. I promise you," Grandma patted his leg.
"You'll have to stay off your feet for a few weeks, but
you will walk again."

"Oh, Babushka, I was so scared!" Archie let the tears
flow at last. "A couple more inches with that plow and
I wouldn't have a foot. I sure am lucky!"

"Luck? No, child, it wasn't luck. You'd better be
thanking the saints." Grandma looked up at the bright
icon above her bed and crossed herself. "Somebody
was watching over you, boy. Now, I got to go and
finish making those dumplings."

When she was gone Archie stared at the picture of
the Virgin Mary in her elaborately painted metal box.
The flickering light of the candle burning on the shelf in
front of the icon made the eyes of the Virgin seem to
open and close.

*Did the Virgin Mary keep the plow from cutting off my
foot?* Archie wondered. *Was it one of the other saints?
Could it have been an angel? Was there really a God
somewhere who watched over people? Did He care about a
stubborn, rebellious teenager who would not speak to his
father?*

Archie crossed himself and closed his eyes. All his

life he had bowed before the family icons without really considering what they meant. He had gone to church on Sundays and holy days like everyone else in the village. He made his routine confessions to the priest because that was the thing to do. It had never made a difference in his life. Not until today had he come face to face with the question of whether or not it was real. Did God exist? Did He care about Archie? The more Archie considered these questions, the dizzier he became. At last the questions stopped whirling in his head. He seemed to be rising higher and higher. Then darkness. Archie slept.

* * *

In spite of Grandmother's herbal poultice, Archie's foot was slow to heal. For three weeks he was confined to the house, unable to move without help.

One sultry summer morning Babushka placed a bench outside near the back door. "Come sit in the sun while I go to market," she said, placing an arm around Archie's waist, coaxing him to stand.

"You're doing fine!" she encouraged as he hopped along beside her to the bench. "Now don't you run away. I'll be back quick as a cat can wink its eye."

Archie leaned against the whitewashed wall and stretched his lame leg on the wooden bench. Through narrowed eyelids he watched life in the village go by. Farmers cut neat furrows between low green rows of corn. Carefree boys splashed and yelled in the river swimming hole. Women called to each other as they spread their clothes to dry on the riverbank. Teenage girls, baskets in hand, skipped across the fields in search of mushrooms. A procession of gaily dressed neighbors went laughing down the road on their way to a wedding.

Zenya and Bert played tag in the yard. Mary scattered corn for the chickens. Mother swept the hard earth smooth around her doorstep. Roman burst from the house, fishing pole in hand.

"Hey, Roman," Archie called. "Where are you going?"

"Where do you think? Fishing, of course. Too bad you can't come!" Roman stopped in front of Archie, waving the pole before his face.

"Oh, shut up. You think you're so smart."

"What are you so mad about? It's your own fault you got hurt."

"What do you mean? It was an accident and you know it."

"I mean it serves you right for leaving home. Papa says God punishes children for disobeying their parents and that's why you got hurt with the plow. So there!" Roman turned and ran out the gate and across the field toward the river.

Archie clenched his fists and hit the bench. He drew a quick breath and grimaced as his bad leg slid to the ground with a painful thud. He closed his eyes and bit his lip. Life was not fair. Why was everything going wrong? Why did he have that accident when he was trying so hard to prove himself? Was God really punishing him for leaving home? Then why did Babushka say the saints were looking after him? Had he not been right in refusing to buy the vodka? Would things never work out? Why was life so confusing? The heat within matched the hot rays of the sun falling on his slumped figure.

Then the heat lessened as though a cloud had suddenly overshadowed him. He opened his eyes to find Domka Shipowick looking down at his tousled head. The love and understanding he read in his mother's eyes momentarily cooled the steam that was building within. "Hi, Mamma," he said.

"I know it's hard not being able to go fishing," she said.

"Yeh. But it's worse not being able to work."

"I know." Mrs. Shipowick propped her broom against the wall and sat on the bench beside him. "I wish you'd come back home. We miss you."

"I can't." Archie stared at the toes of his good foot as they made circles in the dust.

"What can't you do? Forgive your father?"

"He had no right to do what he did."

"He couldn't help himself. He was drunk. He loves you, Archie, just as much as I do."

"Funny way to show it. Besides, I'm old enough to make my own way. I don't need him."

"Oh, Archie." Mother sounded hurt and disappointed.

Archie sighed and stared out across the undulating fields to a rise in the distance where the landlord's house was now partially hidden by cherry and apple orchards in full leaf.

He could see himself living in a house like that someday. Yes, that was it. He would be a landlord with a happy family gathered around him. He would not drink vodka nor beat his wife and children. He would care for his mother, too. Archie's eyes sparkled at the thought. "Mamma, see Ivan's place over there?"

"Yes."

"Well, someday I'll have a place like that. I'll have lots of money and I'll buy you dresses and dishes and lots of fine things. I won't drink vodka nor beat my kids. My boys won't want to run away."

Mrs. Shipowick sat for a long while, looking at the landlord's house. A horse-drawn carriage rolled along the road toward the rise. Swallows soared and dove around the barn. That was another life over there—one she never dared dream for herself or her family.

"An apple doesn't fall far from the apple tree," she said at last.

"What's that supposed to mean?" Archie asked, turning to look at his mother's serious face.

"I mean it's no use dreaming, son. Your father is a peasant and his father before him. You, too, will work for the landlord. That's the way it's always been. That's the way it's going to be. You will be just like your father."

She stood then, picked up her broom, and walked back into the house.

Archie began drawing circles again in the dust, while the words his mother had spoken made circles in his brain. "An apple doesn't fall far from the apple tree. . . . You will be just like your father."

Archie pushed himself up on one leg. Leaning against the house for support, he hopped to the corner, where he could get a better view of the landlord's farm.

"This apple is going to fall where he wants," Archie said, thrusting forward his chin and straightening his shoulders. "I will not be like my father!"

Home Again

It was cherry picking time before Archie was able to return to work at Ivan's. All during those weeks of waiting for his foot to heal, Archie had refused to go back home or to even speak to his father. "I'll show them how far my apple can roll," he chanted as he picked the dark red cherries. "I'll show them! I don't have to be like my father." His desire to escape the fate of his father kept him going summer and winter, springtime and harvest for two years. However, his sixteenth birthday found him no nearer his goal of becoming a landlord than before he started. In two years he had proved nothing except the fact that he was working for the landlord just like his father and his grandfather before him.

"I'll never get anywhere at this rate," Archie admitted to his friend Alex one sparkling spring Sunday as they hiked along the Dniester River. "It appears that Mamma is right. There's no hope of escape from the power of the landlord. I can't bear the thought of ending up like my father, making everyone suffer while I drown my troubles in vodka."

Violets and buttercups vied for the youths' attention and lost. Mallards and pintails, back from their winter in India, did no better. Engrossed in talk about their common plight, Archie and Alex were oblivious to the cries of the swallows announcing the approach of summer.

"I know what you mean," Alex returned. "We work like slaves six days a week for the landlord and what do we get?"

"I'm sick of it." Archie picked up a stick and used it to beat the grass along the path. "I've a good notion to quit and go to Odessa. I've heard they pay dock hands well."

"I wouldn't if I were you. My cousin went there and found the dockmasters worse than the landlord. Besides, it costs more to live in the city and the streets aren't safe at night."

"What am I supposed to do?" Archie demanded. "Rot here in Podolsk while the landlord gets richer? No way! I'm not going to spend the rest of my life working for Ivan!"

"I've heard there is plenty of work in Romania. They pay well and we'd be closer to home. I'd say that's our best bet."

"Sounds good to me," Archie agreed. "Let's do it."

The rest of the afternoon was spent talking excitedly about Romania and their plans to hike through the Carpathian Mountains, which lay some 30 miles south-west of the river.

That night, over a steaming bowl of borscht, he told Babushka about his plans to leave immediately for Romania.

"I know this is my chance, Babushka," Archie exclaimed. "I'll finally be able to get ahead. I can hardly wait."

"Better wait awhile," Grandma said, ladling more beet soup into the hungry boy's bowl. "Your father is leaving for Canada. Don't you think you ought to make up before he goes? You never know what might happen."

"Good riddance" is what Archie felt like saying, but he took a big bite of rye bread and cheese instead. When his mouth was empty the cruel words were gone. "How soon does he leave?" he asked.

"Three weeks, I think. Oh, here comes your mother now."

Mrs. Shipowick pushed open the door. Her eyes were bright and her cheeks were flushed. Going straight to the table she sat down beside Archie and covered his left hand with both of hers. Speaking directly to him, she said, "Archie, you must come home. Your father is leaving for Canada in three weeks. He got his ticket just today. Those who have gone before say it is wonderful over there. You can have land free just for going and farming it. The soil is rich and everyone is a landlord. He says he'll make lots of money and send for us. But, oh, Archie, what if something happens to him?" Mrs. Shipowick's voice broke as she continued. "I can't bear for him to go with this thing between you two. Please come home and let's be happy together for the few days we have left."

"But, Mamma, you know how I feel about Papa."

"Archie, please, for my sake, come home now. For two years you have not spoken to your father. It is enough. He doesn't want to go with things this way, but he is too proud to make the first move. You are the oldest son. It is your place to care for the family when he goes. Please, I beg you, come back home now. It will mean so much to me."

Archie knew his mother spoke the truth. It had been long enough. If he was to take over as head of the Shipowick household, then he must begin right away by making things as easy for his mother as possible. "Yes, Mamma, I'll come," he said, placing a kiss on her tear streaked face. "Don't worry. I'll take care of you."

"Then come now," she insisted. She stood, still holding his left hand. "Come now and eat cabbage rolls with us. I've made poppy seed buns too, just for you."

As Archie crossed the few yards between Babushka's house and his own he found it easier than he had anticipated. The aromas coming from the kitchen were delightful. He had forgotten, too, how good was the smell of freshly tanned leather.

Archie stood for a moment, drinking in the scene: his father mending a pair of tan leather boots, a half empty bottle of vodka on the bench beside him; Mary, Roman, Bert, and Zenya already seated at the table, looking at him expectantly; his mother dishing up cabbage rolls; the warm glow of the candles. It was as if after two years he had walked back into the room and everything was as he had left it. There was even a place set for him at the table.

"We're ready," Mrs. Shipowick said, looking anxiously towards her husband and then towards her son who still stood in the doorway as if transfixed by an unseen force.

Mr. Shipowick took off his leather apron and laid it across the worktable. Slowly, deliberately, he walked to the basin under the window and washed his hands. At last he took his place at the head of the table. Only then did he look at Archie.

Time seemed to reel backwards as their eyes locked. Archie's knees felt weak. A deep, dark bitterness began churning in the middle of his stomach. How could he forget the flashing blue anger those eyes had shown the night he'd refused to buy the vodka. Archie blinked trying to shut out the picture of that awful night. When he opened them again his father's eyes had softened, his jaws were relaxed.

Nodding his head toward the empty place, Mr.

Shipowick said gruffly, "Sit down, Archie."

Archie sat down, grateful that the confrontation was over. Mary smiled at him across the table. Roman jabbed him with his elbow. Zenya winked at him, and Bert said, "I'm glad you're home."

"Bow your heads for the blessing, children," Mother spoke softly.

As Archie closed his eyes and listened to the ancient Slavic blessing, the horrible sickening feeling vanished and in its place a warm glow seemed to envelop his body, making him feel a part of the family again. It was good to be home.

After the blessing, everyone began talking at once.

"How far is Canada?"

"How will you get there?"

"Will you be back for Christmas?"

"Can we go, too?"

"Shush, children," Mrs. Shipowick warned. "Your father has worked hard today. Let him eat in peace."

"Yes, Mamma." Five pairs of eyes stared at the cabbage rolls on their plates, but no one raised a fork. How could they eat when they were bursting with questions?

At last Mary took a bite of the meaty stuffed cabbage roll that had simmered in tomato sauce until it was tender and juicy. Roman followed her example. Archie felt a gentle push against his shins. Mary was looking at him and frowning. He picked up a slice of dark bread and spread it with Mamma's thick, white garlic flavored cheese. He laid strips of dill pickles across the bread and took a big bite. "Mamma, you are still the best cook in the world," Archie said. "Babushka is all right, but I'd rather have you any day!"

"I want a sandwich like yours," Bert said, shoving a slice of bread along the table to Archie.

"All right, I'll make you one."

As the meal continued Archie couldn't help comparing this night with the evening he had left home. On the surface things seemed just the same. Furniture, dishes, and tableware remained unchanged. However, family members, though sitting in their usual places, had changed considerably. Zenya's feet no longer dangled from the bench but were placed firmly on the floor. Bert's chubby baby face was gone. His whole body had lengthened into a smaller version of Roman, who was now almost as tall as Archie. Mary was more mature and self-controlled than he remembered. Mother was a bit plumper. There was a showing of gray behind Father's ears. Two years ago Archie's own voice had been high. Now it was lower, more like his father's.

"I'm going with Alex to Romania," Archie said, not because it fit into the conversation, but because he needed to hear himself so he could compare his voice with his father's.

Domka Shipowick dropped her fork and stared at him in disbelief, her eyes watering. "Who will look after us with your father gone to Canada? You are the eldest. I was counting on you to be the man of the house after Father goes."

"I know, Mamma," Archie squirmed. He felt his face grow hot at the mention of his new role. "Romania isn't far, not like Canada. The border is just a good day's hike from here."

"Why must you go?" Mrs. Shipowick asked.

"I can't possibly provide for you and the family by working at Ivan's," Archie replied, pleased with his quick response. "I'll never get ahead here. I've heard times are good in Romania. The farmers need workers and they pay well."

"Glad to see you're using your head for something besides a hat rack," Samuel Shipowick said. He wiped his mouth on the back of his hand and pushed away from the table. "The czar has promised to do something about the farming situation, but his reforms have helped very little. It's true, what the boy says. There's no chance for a peasant in this country."

"Is that why you're going to Canada, Papa?" asked Roman.

"You bet it is! 'A nightingale sings sweetest when it's free,' my father used to say. I've waited long enough for freedom from the landlord. I'm not getting any younger. So I figured when the chance came to go to Canada, I ought to take it."

"What's it like over there?" Archie leaned forward. He wanted to know more about this mysterious land across the blue ocean, beyond the mountains, where he himself might go someday.

"It's a rich, fertile land—flat and rolling, a lot like the Ukraine. The difference is that there are hundreds of miles of unsettled steppes, prairies they call them over there. The government is giving the land away to anyone who will farm it. If old Pete can make a go of it, I can, too. There I can be my own boss and no one will tell me what to do."

"But, Samuel, it's so far away," sighed Mrs. Shipowick, as she began stacking the soiled plates.

"It won't be for long, Domka. I'll build a house and make lots of money. I'll send for you and the children. You'll live like Ivan's missus, riding around in carriages in all your finery." Mr. Shipowick's leathery face broke into a wide grin. "You'll have lace curtains and china dishes. No doubt about it."

Mrs. Shipowick looked fondly at her husband and then at her eldest son. As she took Archie's plate she whispered, "Where have I heard that before?"

Archie remembered the promise he had made to her when he was recovering from his accident. Perhaps

Babushka was right. He was a lot like his father. Both of them had a quick temper. Both were strong willed and determined. Both were restless, dissatisfied with life as they knew it. Life outside of Russia beckoned to father as well as to son.

Maybe that's why we have such a hard time getting along. Archie chewed on the side of his mouth as he tried out this thought. *Something like magnets. Opposite poles attract and like poles repel.*

"Papa," Archie said, suddenly remembering something his mother had said two years before. "Do you believe that apples always fall near the apple tree?"

Mr. Shipowick tapped his fingers on the table several times before replying. "In Canada they don't. Here they do."

"Then I want to go to Canada too," Archie begged. "Take me with you. I'd work hard."

"Take's money" was all Samuel Shipowick said, but Archie knew that meant no. For a moment he had dared to hope it might be possible. He should have known better than to ask. They never had enough for necessities, let alone savings for a trip to Canada. His father had borrowed the money for his ticket from a neighbor. Archie would have to wait. For a moment he felt the old anger returning. If his father hadn't spent so much money on vodka there might have been enough money for him to go. Not wanting an argument on his first night back home, he squelched the cutting words. Instead, he suggested, "If you'll send for me first, then I could help you earn money for the others."

"Hmmph! We'll see about that." Samuel stood, putting an end to the conversation. In a moment he was back at his workbench cutting out another pair of boots.

"I'm going to Babushka's to get my clothes," Archie said, rising. "I'll be back soon."

Once outside, he walked past Grandma's cottage to the place where he could see Ivan's house glistening like silver in the moonlight. A warm wind breathed across the land bringing to him the soft, sensuous scent of lilacs.

"I'll plant lilacs by my house in Canada." Archie grinned as he thought of what life would be like in that country where anyone could be a landlord. He could hardly wait to get to that promised land where apples didn't fall near the apple tree . . . where a boy didn't have to grow up to be like his father simply because he was born his son. In Canada he could be anything he chose. There his dreams would surely come true.

"Canada! Here I come!" Archie flung both hands towards the sky, shouting his promise to the man in the moon.

First Drink

O n the morning of June 22, 1911, Archie Shipowick awoke in time to hear old Vasili's rooster
announce the first day of summer; it was also to
be Archie's first day as head of the Shipowick household. Today Samuel Shipowick would leave for Canada, and he, Archie Shipowick, would be totally re-
sponsible for the six Shipowicks of Podolsk village. The
thought sent him bounding out of bed. No one else was
awake.

Archie shivered as he dressed, for the sun was not
yet up and the air was cool and crisp. He tiptoed past
the sleeping forms of his brothers and sisters, ex-
hausted from the excitement of the night before. It
seemed everyone in the village had come by to drink to
Samuel Shipowick's health and good fortune for his
long journey. It was past midnight when the candles
were blown out and they had settled down to sleep.

In the half light of dawn Archie found his way to the
front room where his father's canvas bags, already
packed, waited patiently by the door. The cobbler's
bench, now cleared of leather and tools, looked forlorn;
an overturned vodka bottle in the center.

Impulsively, Archie reached for the bottle and lifted
it to his nose and breathed deeply. The smell brought

back memories of his father through the years, some bitter like the smell of the vodka, but others sweet and joyous. He thought of Easter, when Father rolled eggs with them; and Christmas, when they went through the streets of the village singing carols and eating and drinking in each other's houses. He remembered how proud he always was at weddings and feast days when his father was the center of attraction. He could see him now, laughing, dancing, leaping into the air, and clicking his heels together. He remembered sitting close to his father during Mass to keep warm on cold winter mornings, and the ecstasy he'd experienced as a child when Samuel had thrown him high into the air and caught him. For the first time he realized how much he would miss his father, in spite of their misunderstandings. Somehow he wished he could hold all those lovely, beautiful memories forever. In his desire to capture them, Archie lifted the bottle to his lips and drank the remains of his father's vodka.

It was awful. The bitter liquid stung his throat. *Yuk! How can Papa drink this stuff?* Archie made a face at the empty bottle in his hand.

Replacing the bottle carefully on the table so as not to awaken the others, he tiptoed over to stand by the still warm stove. Opening the door, he held his hands over the coals. Then taking a piece of kindling he stirred the embers and added a few sticks of wood. He blew on the coals and they burst into flames. As they did it seemed there was an answering fire in his stomach. The tingling, warm sensation spread outward from the middle of his body until he felt a sense of warmth and well-being all over. He thought it must be the vodka. He quietly closed the door of the stove and tiptoed to the back door.

He went outside and closed the door carefully behind him. He stood on the top step and let the first rays of the morning sun fall on his face. "Maybe vodka isn't so bad after all," Archie said to the chickens that were pecking at his feet. "After all, every grown man I know drinks, even Father Gorbenko, the priest. I guess I'll be expected to drink once in a while, too, at parties and stuff like that. I could do that and still not get drunk."

Archie walked across the courtyard to the side of Babushka's cottage, where the wild roses were already blooming on the fence. The early morning sun caught in the dew drops making them sparkle like silvery diamonds on the pale pink petals. Archie could smell the light, sweet perfume of the roses, like the scent Ivan's missus wore to church.

"I'll buy a bottle of perfume for Mamma when I'm a land owner," Archie promised himself. "In fact I'll probably be so rich that I'll buy her three bottles, one that smells like roses, one like lilacs, and the other like the lilies of the valley that grow by Ivan's house."

Archie raised his eyes to look at the landlord's mansion, silhouetted against the bright pinks and golds of the morning sky. Spreading his arms as if to embrace the whole countryside, Archie stuck out his chest and with a defiant gleam in his eyes said, "I'm going to be richer than you ever thought of being, Ivan. My lands will stretch for miles across the Canadian prairies. I'll build a house fit for a czar." Archie grinned at the thought.

"Archie!" His mother stood in the open doorway waving two wooden buckets. "Bring some water and come for breakfast."

"All right, Mamma. I could eat a horse!" He grabbed the buckets and sprinted to the well. He fastened the well rope to the handle of one bucket with a square knot he knew would hold, and threw the bucket into the well. The weight of the bucket unwound the rope from the roller until the bucket splashed into the water far below. Carefully, Archie turned the handle of the windlass, bringing the water to the top. He filled the empty bucket at his feet, then dropped the first bucket into the well again. *I don't suppose they have wells like this in Canada,* Archie thought. *Probably everyone has one of those fancy new windmills that pumps the water up for you.*

Archie carried the two buckets of ice-cold water into the kitchen and set them by the washstand. He splashed some of the water into a basin and washed his face and hands.

"Sit down, Archie, we're waiting for you." His father spoke impatiently, but Archie seemed not to notice. His mind was on Canada and wind-operated pumps, fancy houses, carriages, and perfume.

"I wish you were staying until Saturday, Samuel," Domka Shipowick said as she placed a platter of fried strips of cornmeal mush and bacon in the center of the table. "You'll miss St. John's feast. You're always the life of the party. No one can dance the *hopak* as well as you."

"Nor the *pereplyas,*" added Mary. "You are always the winner. No one can jump as high, nor move as quickly as you."

"It's not going to be any fun without you," Zenya's chin began to quiver.

"Nonsense!" laughed Samuel. "Archie can do as well. Didn't you see how he danced at Michael's wedding? I expect Archie to take my place at the feast. All of you must be there to cheer him on."

"All right, Papa," Bert said. The others nodded and began to eat. The rest of the mealtime was spent in excited talk about Canada and all the presents Samuel promised to send them. Babushka joined the family for a cup of coffee. No one seemed anxious for the meal to end. At last Samuel stood and said, "Well, it's time I was going. See that you mind Mamma. Archie, you're in charge."

He picked up his bags and walked out of the house, stopping for a moment at the gate to give each a hug.

"I'll never see you again," Babushka stated matter of factly.

"I have a feeling I won't either," said Domka Shipowick as she watched her husband stride down the road toward the west.

Archie's knees trembled as he watched his father's figure get smaller and smaller and at last disappear around the bend in the road beyond a clump of trees. For a moment he held on to the gate to steady himself. He felt sick at his stomach. No, not here. He was in charge. Six Shipowicks were counting on him. He swallowed hard and straightened his shoulders, taking in a deep breath of the fragrant June air.

"Oh, Archie," Domka Shipowick turned to her eldest son, sobbing.

Archie put his arms around her and held her close. "It's all right, Mamma." He was surprised to find his voice steady, his legs firm. "I'm here. I'll look after you 'til Papa sends tickets for us. Everything will be fine. And I'll dance the hopak for you tomorrow, I promise."

"Oh, goodie!" cried Zenya. "I'm going to tell Maria."

"Not before you help Mary wash the breakfast dishes," ordered Archie. "And you get back here, Bert," he called to the younger boy who was just disappearing around the corner of the house. "You and Roman are going to help me chop and stack wood."

"I don't want to chop wood," Roman grumbled. "I want to go fishing."

"Do as your brother says," Domka Shipowick patted him on the back. "Archie is in charge now."

Yes, Archie was in charge and he liked how it felt. He would do his best to look after the family, and tomorrow he would dance at the feast of St. John in his father's place.

A special meal was planned for the day following the dance. Mary and Zenya helped mother make mountains of potato and sauerkraut dumplings; they boiled them and then browned them with onions in the iron skillet until they were golden crisp. They made meaty stuffed cabbage rolls, and rich cheese pancake roll-ups. They baked fresh bread and crunchy honey biscuits.

Roman and Bert kept the woodbox by the kitchen stove filled, carried water, and ran errands. Archie helped Babushka get down the big wooden box from the rafters where they stored clothes worn only for weddings and feast days.

"I can't wait to see you in Samuel's clothes," Babushka said as she quickly rummaged through the clothing, bringing out a pair of black trousers and a light gray, long-sleeved shirt. The shirt, buttoned on the side, was embroidered with black, red, and gold around the collar, sleeves, and hem.

"It took me a whole winter to make this outfit," Grandma continued. Her face was flushed and her eyes had a faraway look as if she were actually seeing back through the years. "It was during the blizzard of '88. Oh, how handsome Samuel looked dancing the hopak, the handsomest man in the village!" Babushka closed her eyes for a moment and sighed. "Ah, well. He's gone now and you must wear the shirt. Here, try it on."

Archie took the cherished garments from her outstretched hands and disappeared into the bedroom. The trousers were loose-fitting, tied with a string around the waist. He tucked the legs into his high-topped felt boots and pulled the shirt over his head. It hung loosely on his thin body, but the length seemed right.

"How do I look, Babushka?" he asked, stepping back into her front room.

"Hmmm," she said, pursing her lips and tilting her head. "It does seem a bit too baggy, but this belt should fix that." She tied a wide red sash around his waist and straightened the gathers of the shirt so that they fell evenly over the black trousers.

"There. Now all you need is this cap and you're ready to dance!"

Archie ran around the little room and leaped into the air in front of Grandma. He raised his right leg and landed on his left, just as he had seen his father do so many times.

"Wonderful!" exclaimed Babushka. "You are wonderful. Just like your father. And how handsome you are! We'll be proud of you at the dance tonight."

That night in the village street in front of the church Archie made them all proud. Mamma and Babushka swayed in time with the accordian music as they watched Archie dance the hopak. The children clapped their hands and stomped their feet to the fast rhythmic beat.

"Oh, Mamma! Just look at Archie!" Mary exclaimed as the boy leaped high in the air, his face golden from the reflection of the large bonfire around which the men dance.

"I know; isn't he grand?" Mamma hugged Mary and Zenya.

"He's nearly as good as Papa, isn't he, Babushka?" asked Roman.

"Every bit as good," Grandma beamed. "He's just like Samuel. Just like his father."

"I hope they do the pereplyas next," said Bert. "I want to see if he can beat the other dancers."

"Of course he will," said Mrs. Shipowick, glowing with pride for her firstborn.

When the hopak was finished someone called for the pereplyas. "Yes! Yes!" the crowd shouted. The accordian player began the melody of a popular tune and five men stepped into the golden circle near the fire: Michael, Alex, Christopher, Gregori, and Archie.

The dance began with a slow rhythm and gradually became stormier. The men formed themselves into two couples, hands on hips, with Archie between them. Then moving forward they flung their arms open and stamped their feet to the rhythm of the music.

Archie leaped into the air; then, making a half turn, he raised his right leg and landed on his left. This was the signal for the challenge. Michael threw himself forward with his arms folded, and Gregori answered him by executing the same movement, turning in the process. Whatever the others did, Archie came back with a performance more startling and beautiful. One minute they were throwing themselves on their knees, flinging their arms back, and the next minute they were stamping their feet with incredible skill and rapidity.

Through every challenge Archie came out the winner. His name was on every girl's lips as they watched his graceful form dodging, leaping, twisting, and turning to the ever faster beat.

All the dancers formed a row for the final routine, in which they jumped into the air, clicking their heels and slapping their knees with the palms of their hands.

"Archie, you were marvelous!" Mary said, throwing her arms around his neck.

"We're so proud of you!" exclaimed Zenya as she hugged his waist.

"You were great!" Roman said, punching his brother a hard one on the shoulder. "Just like Papa."

"Archie!" called Michael. "Come drink with us."

Archie broke away from his family circle to join the men on the way to the tavern.

"You did great, Archie, old boy," commented Gregori, throwing an arm over his shoulder.

"You sure made me think of Samuel," said Ivan. "You even look like him in those clothes."

"A toast to Archie," Michael said, thrusting a glass of vodka into the jubilant youth's hands. For a moment Archie hesitated. He thought of the countless times he'd come to this same tavern to buy liquor for his father. He remembered his resolve never to drink. But then he had already broken that promise yesterday morning and now the men were raising their glasses expectantly. He was a man now. They expected him to be just like his father, full of fun, ready to drink and laugh with the rest. He accepted the glass and drained it, holding it out for a refill.

"Aha!" laughed Christopher. "Not only can he dance like his father, he can drink like him as well!"

The warmth of the vodka reaching up into his brain stilled any misgivings he had. If this was what it took to be a man, then this is what he would do.

The rest of the night was a bit blurred. He woke up the next morning with a sick stomach, a foul mouth, and a splitting head.

"I've made a pot of black coffee for you," Domka Shipowick said. "Drink some. I know it will help."

"Oh, Mamma! I got drunk last night, didn't I? I'm sorry," Archie said, looking up into her sad, dark eyes. "I just couldn't help myself. They all wanted me to drink with them and . . . and . . . well, I wanted so much to be a part of . . ." He hesitated, embarrassed.

"I know," Mrs. Shipowick said, running her hand through his dark brown hair. "You wanted to be part of the men's group. You meant to stop after one or two, but they kept offering you drinks and you couldn't refuse."

Archie looked at his mother in amazement. "That's

exactly how it was, but how did you know? You weren't there."

"I've heard the story often enough from Samuel. You're him all over again, Archie, just like Babushka has always said. An apple doesn't fall far from the apple tree." His mother turned her head to hide her disappointment. When she looked at him again, she was smiling. "You were superb in the dances last night."

Archie reached out his cup for a refill and smiled back at his mother. "I'll always try to make you proud of me," he promised.

"God bless you, son," she replied, crossing herself. "And your father, wherever he is. May the saints watch over him. Yes, I shall always be proud of you, for you are so much like your father. Like him, you are full of fun, strong-willed, and above all a dreamer. Only, I wish you weren't a dreamer. It's through his dreams that I have lost your father and it's through your dreams that I will lose you."

Archie was finished with his coffee. "I've got to see Alex."

"About Romania?" his mother asked.

"Yes," answered Archie on his way out the front door. "I'll see you for lunch after Mass."

Domka spoke something softly to herself as he closed the door. Archie wasn't quite sure, but he thought he heard her say, "He's just like his father!"

Canada Bound

Christmas of 1912 was a time of rejoicing for the Shipowicks of Podolsk village, because Archie was back from Romania.

"The saints be praised! You are home!" Domka Shipowick exclaimed, holding out her arms to welcome her 17-year-old son. "It wouldn't be Christmas without you!"

"Wait until you see the gifts I brought!" Archie's face was radiant as he returned his mother's hug.

"Show us! Show us!" begged Zenya, clapping her hands with excitement.

"What did you get me?" queried Bert.

"I'll never tell," teased Archie. "You'll have to wait . . ."

"Until St. Nicholas Day," finished Mrs. Shipowick.

"Ah, Mamma," complained Roman. "We don't believe in St. Nicholas anymore. We know you and Papa always put the gifts under our pillows. Why can't we have our gifts now?"

"No, not until the sixth of December," insisted Mother. "The time will go by fast enough. It's only a few days."

"Aw, shucks!" said Bert, frowning.

"I can't wait," whined Zenya.

"You'll just have to," replied Mother, firmly.

"I know what doesn't have to wait," suggested Mary, her eyes sparkling.

"What?" chorused the younger children.

"Stories," said Mary. "Archie, tell us about Romania. What's it like?"

"There are more mountains than here," Archie began. He sat down at the kitchen table. Mrs. Shipowick, Babushka, and the children gathered around. "The country is heavily forested with pine and fir and the rivers are swifter than the Dniester. The people are friendly, but they don't talk like us. Their alphabet is different, too."

"What work did you do?" Roman wanted to know.

"Lots of things," replied Archie. "When I first got there it was summer and I weeded cabbages and cauliflowers until I thought my back would break. Later, when the migrant workers had gone, I got a job as a cook for a group of shepherds. That's what I've done for the past year."

"You? A cook?" laughed Mary. "I can't believe it!"

"Well, I was," Archie spoke with pride. "I can make corn meal mush as well as you can and you should taste my borscht!"

During the next few days Archie proved his culinary abilities to his skeptical brothers and sisters by making a pot of beet soup and a pan of corn bread. Evenings were filled with stories and songs he had learned from wandering groups of Romanian gypsies.

What Archie failed to tell them was that he had also learned from the gypsies how to play cards. Gambling and drinking had used up far more money than he cared to admit. It seemed he was destined to follow in his father's footsteps. No matter how many times he had tried to save his money, Archie seemed powerless to stop the downward course of his life.

When at last St. Nicholas Day arrived Zenya, Bert, and Roman climbed out of bed and pulled the covers from their big brother.

"Get up, you sleepy head!" Bert shouted in Archie's ear. "St. Nicholas needs your help!"

Archie burrowed his head under the feather pillow and pretended to snore, but it was a losing battle as the three pulled him, pillow and all, right off the bed.

"All right! All right! Hold your horses."

"We don't have any horses," teased Zenya.

"You know what I mean, young lady," laughed Archie. "Get out of here and let me get dressed." He threw the pillow at his little sister.

Domka Shipowick and Mary already had the corn-meal mush cooked and coffee made by the time Archie dragged his suitcase of surprises into the living room. There were embroidered shawls and bright head scarves for Babushka and Mother. Mary got a fine pair of felt slippers. For Roman and Bert there were hand-crafted leather belts. Zenya was delighted with her Romanian peasant doll. Then he brought out rich, dark slabs of chocolate for everyone.

After breakfast, Mary and Mrs. Shipowick took wal-nuts and apples to a sick neighbor and the children went to the schoolhouse for the annual play. After the play the schoolmaster, dressed as St. Nicholas with a long, white beard, passed out sweets to the good children. He was followed by a mischievious devil who gave dry twigs to the bad boys and girls. Bert got both sweets and a dry twig, much to the delight of his older brothers.

"The days are not long enough!" declared Mrs. Shipowick, as Christmas drew near. "I don't know how we'll get all the baking done."

A 12-course meal must be prepared for the Holy Supper, to be eaten on Christmas Eve as soon as the first star came out. Nuts had to be cracked and a special bread, called *kolach*, baked. This was a sweet, white dough flecked with raisins, braided into an open circle, and glazed with a beaten egg.

On Christmas Eve Mrs. Shipowick spread a white embroidered cloth over the rough wooden table. "It stands for purity," she explained.

Next she placed a three-tiered kolach in the center of the table. "That represents the Trinity," she reminded the five children who had gathered to watch the ceremony.

Babushka set a white beeswax candle in the center of the loaf and lit it. "This is to remind us of the star that shone over the stable in Bethtlehem," she chanted as she had done every Christmas Eve for as long as Archie could remember.

Mother brought a sheef of wheat from the cupboard, tied it with a red ribbon, and placed it in a brown milk pitcher. This she set near the kolach. "For our ancestors," she said.

Mary carefully placed seven plates on the beautiful tablecloth, the extra one for Father, who was celebrating Christmas 10,000 miles away in Canada—alone.

Archie's mouth watered as his mother and Babushka continued placing the traditional foods on the table for supper: *kutia* (boiled whole wheat with honey and poppy seed), borscht (beet soup), stuffed fish (caught that very day by Archie at the village stream), *varenyky* (dumplings) with sauerkraut filling, verenyky with potato filling, verenyky with prune filling, *holubsti* (cabbage rolls) stuffed with rice and mushrooms; peas and sauerkraut, stewed dried apples, peaches, pears, prunes, and poppy seed rolls. Even the landlord would eat no better this night.

Before sitting down to supper Archie walked around the house three times as he had seen his father do, blessing the rooms, the furniture, the people, and even the chickens. He took a piece of bread and honey and gave it to each member of the family to indicate his blessing. He felt nervous in his role as head of the household, but Mrs. Shipowick smiled her approval and he continued more confidently. Then he said grace and they all sat down to enjoy the feast.

As they were finishing supper there was a knock at the door. It was Michael. "Christ is born!" he greeted the family.

"Let us adore Him," the Shipowicks answered in unison.

"We're going caroling. Anybody want to come?"

Mary, Roman, and Archie got up to put on their coats, scarves, and boots.

"May I go?" asked Bert.

"No, not this year," answered his mother. "I need you and Zenya to stay home to help Babushka and me welcome the carolers who come to our house. You can help pass out the food after they sing."

"We'll be back in time for midnight mass," Archie promised as he opened the front door, letting in a swirl of powdery snow.

"Archie, close that door before we all freeze!" his mother said with a wave of her hand.

When they were gone, Babushka sighed. "Makes me think when you and Samuel were young."

"I was so proud of Archie tonight." Mrs. Shipowick's eyes glowed as she spoke. "He did the blessing as well as Samuel."

"Just like Papa," Bert agreed.

"Poor Papa," said Zenya. "All alone away over there in Canada. Do you think we'll be with him by next Christmas?"

A north wind whistled around a little cabin in Meath Park, Saskatchewan, Canada. It whipped the snow before it, piling it in drifts along fence rows and against Samuel Shipowick's door.

"Blow all you want!" Archie's father challenged the storm. "You can't reach me in here!"

Samuel put a pot of borscht and a pan of verenykye on top of the black iron cook stove that heated the two rooms he had built on his homestead. When he had first set foot on his land near the North Saskatchewan River, he had thought it much like the rolling steppes he had left behind in Podolsk. Now he considered it more like Siberia!

He opened the lid of the firebox and shoved in another stick of wood. There were enough logs piled in the corner of the cabin to last several days. More was stacked outside the back door.

He placed a cracked bowl and a spoon on the wooden table he had made. Beside the bowl he placed the kolach Mrs. Kovich had sent over, along with the borscht and verenykye, when he had refused to spend Christmas Eve with them. Next to the kolach he placed a half-full bottle of wine.

Samuel pulled one of the benches close to the stove and waited for the food to warm. He was grateful for neighbors who had shared their Holy Supper with him, but somehow it made him more homesick for the old country. The odor of the soup bubbling on the back of the stove and the fragrant smell of fresh bread brought Domka's face before him. No one could cook like her. How he longed to bring her to this new land to share his cabin and his dreams! After supper he lit a second candle and wrote to his wife.

Ten thousand miles and five weeks later the letter was in Mrs. Shipowick's hands. Her fingers trembled as she broke the seal. The look of Samuel's familiar handwriting made her heart beat faster and her throat feel tight. Tears came unbidden to her eyes. She thrust the long white envelope towards Archie, who stood warming himself by the stove. "Read it. I'm too excited," she said, just above a whisper.

He smoothed out the paper and read:

My Dearest Wife:

Tonight is Christmas Eve. The neighbors invited me to share the Holy Supper with them, but I wanted to be alone to think of you and the children. I have eaten now: borscht, verenykye, and kolach, which Mrs. Kovich sent over with one of the boys.

I have cleared one quarter of my land this past summer and have planted it in winter wheat. The work is slow and hard when I have to work alone. I've had to buy a team of horses, a plow, and other implements, as well as seed. I have not yet been able to save enough money for all of you to come to Canada.

I got a job on the railroad laying ties, but there is no work now because of the cold weather. For the past week it has been 40 below zero, much colder than in Podolsk. My ears froze in the short walk to the outhouse yesterday.

With this letter I'm sending a ticket for Archie. I've had to borrow the money. He can work on the railroad to pay it back. Later, I'll send for Roman and Bert.

I long for the day when all of you can be here with me. Give my love to Babushka. Is Bert doing well in school? What about little Zenya? Are there any proposals for Mary? My love to all.

Samuel

"Oh, Mamma! Do you see this? A ticket to Canada! And here is a note addressed to me."

Dear Archie:

Ivan can give you directions about how to get to Austria. From Vienna you can get a train to Paris, France. From there it is not far to the port where you'll take a boat to Montreal. In Montreal you will get a train to Borden, Saskatchewan. When you arrive in Montreal send a telegram to me at Meath Park. I'll meet the train at Borden. You should start immediately so you can be here for spring work.

Papa

"Why, Mamma! You're crying." Archie laid the letter on the table and sat down beside his mother, placing an arm around her waist. "Please don't cry. Aren't you glad I'm going to Canada? This is my chance!"

"Of course, I'm happy and proud for you, son! I know you'll do well." Mrs. Shipowick dabbed at her eyes with the corner of her faded blue apron. "It's just that I've come to depend on you since Samuel left two years ago. I'll miss you. I might never see you again. Canada is so far away!"

"But, Mamma! I'll work hard to help Papa. We'll save up money for all of you to go to Canada, I promise. You're going to have a fine carriage and beautiful clothes. You'll be a real lady in Canada. Just wait and see!"

Mrs. Shipowick tried to smile for Archie's sake. "I hope you are right. Somehow I just feel it in my bones that I'll never see you nor Samuel again. I can't help it, son. That's just the way I feel."

Archie gave his mother a squeeze and a kiss on her round, tear-stained cheek. "When Archie Shipowick gets to Canada things will really begin to happen! I'm going now to talk to Ivan about my plans."

Archie returned after two hours with a map carefully drawn, showing the best route to travel through Hungary to Austria. He laid it on the table and in the light of the afternoon sun shining through the window he traced his journey for his excited brothers and sisters.

"Ivan says I should start right away," Archie explained. "I need to go before the spring thaw sets in. Roads thick with mud will be hard to travel, and swollen streams will be difficult to cross. If I go now I can walk across on the ice."

"How far is it to Austria?" Roman asked.

"Oh, about 300 miles as the crow flies," answered Archie, "but I'll have to go further than that because of the mountains."

"Will you walk all that way?" asked Zenya, her brow wrinkled into a frown.

"Ivan says I can get a ride on Monday with some people from the next village. They go as far as Beregevo. From there it is just a few miles to the border. He's sure I can get rides now and then with Hungarian farmers going to market. If I'm lucky I could reach Vienna in a week. Otherwise it might take as long as three weeks, depending on the weather."

"May the Holy Mother watch over you," said Mrs. Shipowick with a glance at the picture of the Virgin Mary smiling down at them from the wall above Samuel's old workbench.

For a moment Archie, too, looked up at the smiling face of the mother of Jesus. The flickering candle that always burned on the shelf in front of the picture made her eyes seem to dance as they had that day long ago in Babushka's home when he had been injured.

"The saints watched over me when I was plowing that time in Ivan's field," Archie said. "I'm sure they'll watch over me on my journey to Canada, too. See how the Virgin smiles at me?"

He turned towards the window then, and stared out across the white, windswept fields. At that moment his heart felt as cold and barren as the winter landscape. He didn't want his mother to see the doubt in his eyes. He had spoken those words to reassure his mother. He didn't really believe them. How could the Holy Mother of God care for one so wicked as he? His apple had fallen near the apple tree, all right. Like his father, he was powerless to break the habits of drinking and gambling. He'd done other things, too, in Romania. Things he would be ashamed for his mother to know about. The thought of her love and trust cut through him then like a knife. *I'm one rotten apple; that's what I am!* Archie thought. *I just hope she never finds out how rotten!*

"May the Blessed Virgin smile at you every step of the way," said Mrs. Shipowick, crossing herself. "Come now, put away your map. Supper is ready."

Gambling Man

Amonth later Archie stood on the deck of a French steamer, watching the shoreline of Europe grow smaller, then merge with the mists of the distant horizon. He gripped the railing as if to keep his body from following his mind across the hundreds of miles he had traveled during the past three weeks, back to the muddy roads of Podolsk village and the little white cottage that had been his home for almost 18 years.

He closed his eyes as he pictured the family sitting at the table eating borscht the night before he left. He imagined himself chewing a big hunk of his mother's fresh black bread spread thick with butter and cottage cheese. It seemed he could hear the children's excited chatter and see his mother's dark eyes, swollen and red from weeping, fixed on him with a mixture of pride and sorrow.

Above the hum of the engine and the lapping of the waves he could hear her final words, "Archie, my son! You are brave, just like your father! I am so proud of you, but I am afraid for you too. It is a long journey. I'll pray for you every day that God will keep you safe."

"Well, Mamma," Archie whispered the words into the wind and wished it might carry them to her. "God has answered your prayers so far."

"*Scho ve zniete?* (What do you know?)"

Archie spun around at the sound of his mother tongue. How good it sounded after the last few weeks of trying to communicate with the Hungarians, Austrians, Swiss, and French. He found himself face to face with a blond youth a year or two older than himself, dressed in a dark brown overcoat with a fur hat like his own pulled down over his ears.

"I'm on my way to Canada," Archie replied. "And you?"

"Toronto," answered the stranger. "To which place in Canada are you headed?"

"Saskatchewan. My name is Archie Shipowick from Podolsk village near the Dniester River."

"And I am Dimitri Raganovich from Kiev. Are you traveling alone?"

"Yes. I'm joining my father who has been there two years already."

"My father is still in Kiev," Dimitri replied. "I will stay with my uncle. It's cold up here. Let's go below and have a game of cards. What do you say?"

Soon the two young men were swapping stories of schools and jobs over a deck of cards on Dimitri's bunk bed. Every day for the next two weeks the two Russians played cards, sometimes alone, sometimes with other passengers. At times they placed bets with imaginary sums of money since neither had any real money to put up. Before the voyage was finished Archie had won and lost several imaginary fortunes.

"I'm really getting good at this," Archie bragged one day. "I wish we had real money to put up. I'm sure I'd win."

"Let's play for our hats," suggested Dimitri. So they put their fur hats on the bed and dealt the cards. Archie had an unlucky hand and lost his hat, but Dimitri felt sorry for him and gave it back.

"You're a great guy!" Dimitri said, with one arm around his new friend's shoulders. "I wish you were going to Toronto with me. We'd soon be rich fellows."

"I'm sure I'll find someone to play cards with in Saskatchewan," Archie rubbed his hands together in anticipation of all the silver he'd soon have in his pockets.

When he wasn't playing cards, Archie walked the deck or stood at the railing watching the ever-changing ocean and sky. The gray-green waves cresting and falling only to rise again were a lot like his own emotions. At times he was jubilant about the prospects of a better life in Canada, and at others he was fearful of what life with Father would be like. Would old feelings of anger return? Would his father treat him as a man now? Would he be able to learn English?

On the day they entered the St. Lawrence River, Archie's emotional wave began to crest. The sight of Canadian soil sent his spirits soaring like the sea gulls that circled the ship. Traffic on the great river was exciting. This was nothing like the little boats he had seen on the Dniester River back home. They passed ships from England, Italy, Denmark, and a dozen other countries, carrying cargoes of wheat, lumber, and coal. The wave crested when Archie's ship docked at Montreal and fell as he and Dimitri faced long lines at the customs and immigration shed. He hit another low as he tried to make himself understood.

"*Parlevous Francais?*" people asked at every turn. "*Englais?*" "Do you speak French? English?"

He shook his head. It was all so confusing. Dimitri wasn't much help. Together they tried the few words of French they knew. People were helpful, one man going out of his way to take them to the Central Railway Station, where they found their westbound trains. It was a relief to sit back and relax, letting the iron horse with its clacking wheels carry him to his destination.

"I'm here at last. I'll soon be rich." The wheels seemed to sing. "I'm here at last. I'll soon be rich."

Archie stared out the window at the Quebec countryside. The rolling forest-covered hills and the wide valleys dotted with farms and villages made him think of France. Snow still blanketed the land, but here and there brown patches of earth were showing through where the sun had already begun its springtime work. They passed horsecarts making ruts in the muddy road just as they did in Podolsk every spring. He noticed pussy willows growing along the track and he wondered if the pussy willows were blooming down by the river behind his village in Podolsk. Probably they were, and Mary would have picked some branches already and brought them into the house, setting them in a jar on the kitchen table.

There was so much to see in this new land, but Archie's eyelids dropped. The rhythmic sway of the train combined with the chanting of the wheels to make him drowsy. He yawned, stretched his legs, and slept.

Archie awoke several hours later to find all signs of spring had vanished. Farms, towns, and roads had also disappeared.

Wilderness. Desolation. Emptiness. Archie searched for the right word to describe the land through which his train rumbled for two days and nights. It was still winter in northern Ontario. Once when they stopped at a lonely station Archie heard wolves howling in the darkness, but there were no signs of people. Did no one live in this wide, lonesome land? Could anyone live in such a place? It was colder than Archie could remember. "Thirty-five degrees below zero," the conductor said. "Unusual for this time of year."

Sudbury, Port Arthur, Kenora, Winnepeg, Saskatoon. The still frozen prairies stretched like a dirty white sheet as far as Archie could see. The stark landscape was broken here and there by a cluster of trees or farm buildings.

The sun was bright, the sky blue, and the air dry. To breathe was like swallowing a knife, and when you exhaled it looked like puffs of smoke that hung in the still, cold air.

"What are those tall wooden towers?" Archie asked the conductor near the end of the second day. "They seem to be at every stop now."

"Grain elevators," answered the conductor. "That's where the farmers bring their wheat. It's stored there until it can be sent by train to markets in the East."

After that the wide expanse of the prairies didn't seem so desolate. Archie looked for the elevators and knew that out beyond those wooden towers were farmers who filled them with wagonloads of grain. He pictured the land golden with rippling fields of wheat as he had seen back in Russia and felt better about this land that was to be his home.

Finally the train puffed into the Borden station. It wasn't much of a town: a church, the grain elevators, a country store, a post office, a tavern, a blacksmith shop, and a few ramshackle houses with snow drifted up around them.

On the station platform stood a lone man with a heavy fleece-lined parka almost hiding his bearded face. His dark pants were stuffed into heavy work boots. He stood there, feet apart, blowing clouds of steam into his cupped hands as his steel blue eyes anxiously scanned the doors of the slowing train.

Archie recognized Samuel at once. He jumped from the still moving train and ran to his father, throwing his arms about him in a bear hug.

Samuel led his son to the front of the station, where a sleigh and a team of horses stood blowing and stamping.

"How are Mamma and Babushka?" asked Samuel when they were seated snugly in the sleigh with the heavy woolen blankets pulled up around their chins and tucked in around them to keep out the cold.

Archie burrowed his feet into the thick layer of straw on the floor of the sleigh and answered, "They are well. Roman has a job at the landlord's. Mary, Zenya, and Bert send their love."

"How was your trip? What do you think of Canada?"

"The trip was fine. Everything went just as you said it would. And Canada? I think it's a great country . . . so wide and so free! The people are friendly, even though I don't speak their language. In Montreal a man walked all the way from the docks to the railway station to show me where to get my train."

"Yes," Mr. Shipowick agreed. "People are like that in this land. Good people. Many are here from Russia." He pointed to the turrets and domes of an Orthodox Church silhouetted against the sky. We'll stay with a Ukranian family tonight and finish the trip tomorrow. It's nearly a hundred miles, too much for one day in this weather."

"Do you have a job for me yet?" Archie asked, his voice muffled by the ice crystals that were already forming on the scarf he had pulled over his mouth.

"That I do," Samuel nodded. "On the railroad with me. I spoke to the foreman just last week. They are hiring a new crew for the spring. We'll start as soon as the thaw begins."

"Doing what?"

"Blocking railroad ties."

"I'll work hard," Archie promised. And he did. It was back breaking work, but the pay was good.

"Just look at all this money!" Archie exclaimed on his first payday. He laid the money on his father's table and counted the strange bills again and again. He folded it and put it in his pocket, but every few minutes he took it out to admire.

"Money is for spending," Archie said at last. "Father, I'm going to the tavern to meet some of the other guys. I'll see you later."

"Bring me a bottle when you come," said Mr. Shipowick. "I could use a drink myself."

Every Saturday was much the same. Archie couldn't wait to get paid so he could go to town for a drink. He took along a pack of cards and gambled for drink and sometimes for money. He lost more than he won, but he felt sure that next week he'd be lucky and win it back. But next week he'd lose again and go home drunk and penniless.

"Why are you doing this?" Samuel Shipowick pounded the table one night when Archie had come staggering home with empty pockets.

"Ha!" Archie spat on the floor. "Look who's talking. I've seen you drunk plenty of times. And don't tell me you've never gambled. I know better. What more do you expect of me? An apple can't fall far from the apple tree!"

"At least I know when to stop!" bellowed his dad. "I borrowed money so I could come here. I haven't repaid that loan. I borrowed money for your ticket, too. I expected you to help, not act like this. I should have left you in the old country to rot!"

"All right! All right!" Archie held up both hands to stop the flood of angry words. "I'll stop. No more drinking. No more gambling." He stood, holding on to the table to steady himself, then stumbled across the room and fell on the bed, face down.

It's true, Archie told himself. *I am just like my father*

. . . *only worse.* It seemed like only yesterday that he had refused to buy vodka for his father. He had vowed then never to touch alcohol. He didn't want to be like his father, but the old man's character seemed to be stamped on every cell of his body. He had no strength to be different, but somehow he had to try. "I'll quit! I swear to God I'll quit," Archie mumbled into the covers.

Fire Escape

The next morning Archie sat on the edge of his bed and stared at the floor. He had to get up and go to work, but his head was splitting. He had vowed last night he would not drink again, but right now, this moment, he had to have a drink. He reached under his pillow and pulled out the bottle he always kept there, took a swallow, corked the bottle, and replaced it carefully under his pillow. Tomorrow he would quit drinking, but tomorrow he needed a drink, too. Then he lost his railroad job and he needed alcohol to get up courage to look for work. Soon his money was gone.

"You've got to get a job!" Samuel Shipowick insisted. "I'm not paying for you to lie around the house and drink! Besides, I've booked a ticket for Roman to come to Canada and you've got to help pay for it!"

Before Roman arrived Archie found work as a hired hand with Rampal Abraham, a German-Russian Baptist. Archie was glad when Roman found work with a Ukranian farmer a few miles down the road.

From sunup until sundown Archie drove a team of four horses as he had done for Ivan back in Podolsk. He worked hard all week and was glad he didn't have to work on Sunday. He took his pay to the village and gambled, drank, and danced until after midnight. Roman sometimes joined him, but when it came to drinking he was no match for his older brother. Archie woke up every Monday morning with a sick stomach, a headache, and a cloudy mind.

"I don't want to plow today," Archie said to himself as he got dressed early one summer morning. "But I've got to go or I might lose my job." He stumbled out to the horses and got them harnessed. Somehow it seemed to take twice as long to get the straps in place on Monday mornings.

Once out of sight of the farmhouse, Archie tied the horses to a poplar tree and lay down to sleep off his hangover.

"Something fishy is going on with Archie," Rampal told his wife soon after Archie had gone. "He works well every day except Monday. He gets almost nothing accomplished on Mondays. Today I'm going to follow him to see what he does."

His wife looked up from kneading bread dough. "I hear he drinks a lot on Sundays at the tavern," she said.

"You're probably right," Rampal agreed as he put on his hat and went out the door in search of Archie.

He found his hired hand snoring under a large poplar tree about a mile from home, the horses contentedly munching grass nearby.

"Archie, wake up!" Mr. Abraham shook the boy's shoulders.

Archie groaned, rolled over, and sat up. The world seemed a merry-go-round of trees, horses, and a man who looked like his boss. He took a deep breath and his mind cleared enough for him to recognize that it was indeed Mr. Abraham and he was not happy.

"I'm sorry, sir," Archie said, staring at the grass at his feet.

"What's wrong?" Mr. Abraham asked. "Are you sick?"

"Yah, I'm sick," admitted Archie. "My head feels like someone took a meat chopper to it and my stomach feels like it's full of rocks."

"Hmmm! I see!" Mr. Abraham frowned for he could smell liquor on Archie's breath. The boy hadn't bothered to shave or wash his face. His hair was uncombed.

Mr. Abraham's anger changed to pity as he looked at the disheveled boy. "Do you have a Bible?" he asked.

"No, sir," Archie replied, not sure what that had to do with his aching head.

"Then I'll give you one tonight when you come in for supper." Mr. Abraham stood, turned to go, then wheeled to face Archie who was trying to pull himself up. "And I want you to take the Bible and go to the Baptist church on Sunday. It'll do you good."

"Yes, sir," Archie replied, willing to do anything to keep his job. "I'll be there." And he was, but on the way home he couldn't resist stopping at the tavern. Sunday church followed by a wild night at the tavern became a regular pattern for Archie in the months that followed. He went to church to please his boss and to the tavern to please himself, or perhaps more accurately to satisfy the demon that seemed to be within him craving for more alcohol.

One Sunday night the home brew served at the tavern was especially good. Archie refilled his glass a dozen times. In the early morning hours he staggered into the barn, not wanting to wake the Abrahams. He felt his way along the wall, past the saddles and harnesses, the rakes and hoes, to the ladder that led to the loft. Not trusting his balance, he climbed the ladder on his knees and fell sprawling in the soft, sweet hay.

Sleep would not come. The liquor was working on his stomach and brain as it had never worked before.

Every inch of his intestines seemed to be on fire. His whole body was burning. He opened his eyes and he imagined he saw flames leaping and dancing around him. He writhed in agony. Was the barn on fire or was he in hell? He tried to raise his head to get out of the terrible inferno, but he could not.

"Oh, God!" he screamed. "I'm going to die! Save me!" Archie's breath was coming in short gasps. Beads of sweat lay on his forehead. "Get me out of this fire and I'll become a Christian. Don't let me die and I'll never drink again. Save me and I'll live for you." Then all was black.

The next morning Archie woke in the hayloft, clear-headed and shivering. There was no sign of the fire of the night before, but it had been so real that Archie would vividly remember that night as long as he lived.

The next Sunday a very sober Archie sat in the wooden pews of the country Baptist church. Bible in hand, he listened intently to the message, hoping for something that would give him the strength to keep his promise to God.

"You are a sinner bound for hell!" the minister was saying. "You were born a sinner. You can't help yourself, your evil desires were passed on to you from your parents. Sin is in your blood. Try as you might you can't change your ways. Some of you have tried a thousand times and failed. You know what I'm talking about!"

He's sure enough talking about me, Archie thought. *I know I shouldn't drink and gamble, but I am powerless to change. How many times I have promised myself to quit drinking, only to succumb to the demon inside me. If someone offered me a drink right now, I'd probably take it.*

"Listen to these words from the prophet Jeremiah, chapter 13, verse 23." The minister held up his open Bible. There was a rustle of pages as people found the place. Archie didn't even try to find the passage. He wasn't sure he knew where to find Jeremiah. Besides, he was afraid that if he took his eyes off the minister he might miss something important.

" 'Can the Ethiopian change his skin, or the leopard his spots?' " The preacher paused a moment and looked in Archie's direction. " 'Then may ye also do good, that are accustomed to do evil.' "

The minister closed his Bible and began pacing the platform. "No, you cannot change your wicked ways, because you were born wicked. You are rotten to the core, evil through and through." He turned a few pages in his Bible and read, " 'The heart is deceitful above all things, and desperately wicked.' "

That's me. Archie sighed at the apparent hopelessness of his condition. *I'm wicked to the core . . . one rotten apple.*

"But don't despair," the preacher seemed to be looking at Archie again. "There is hope! God will take you just as you are. He wants your wicked, evil heart. If you will surrender it to Him now, He will give you a new heart, a clean heart, a pure heart, one that loves to do right. One that will follow Him. Surrender to Jesus now, and you will be born again. The blood of Jesus Christ can cleanse you from all your sins. Look to Him and be saved. Come to Him and live. Come now to the altar and the miracle will happen! Just as you are, come to Jesus."

Archie began to weep as people around him sang softly:

> Just as I am, without one plea
> But that Thy blood was shed for me
> And that Thou bid'st me come to Thee,
> O Lamb of God, I come, I come.

Archie made his way to the front and knelt at the altar. As his tears flowed he could feel the frustration, the anger, and the sins of his past slip away. It was as though a mighty load had been lifted from his shoulders. The desire for drink was gone! He felt like a new person!

Twenty-one years before, he had been born in Podolsk village in Russia, the son of his earthly father, Samuel Shipowick. On a summer's eve in 1916 in a little country church in Borden, Saskatchewan, Archie was born again; through a miracle of the Holy Spirit he had been made a son of his heavenly Father.

News of Archie's conversion spread like fire in the stubble on a dry, windy day.

"Archie Shipowick got saved last Sunday night!" Plump Ukranian housewives stopped their housework to spread the news by telephone to their neighbors on the party line. "Do you think it will last?"

"Where's Archie?" his cronies asked the next Sunday at the tavern. "We need him for a game of poker!"

"Haven't you heard?" the bartender announced as he wiped the counter. "Archie got religion at the Baptist church last Sunday. I don't reckon he'll come here any more!"

"You've got to be kidding!" a tall Russian named Nick exclaimed as he swaggered up to the bar. "Don't tell me that Archie's got religion!"

"That's what my old woman says," affirmed the bartender. "She heard it from Sarah Wolloch, who saw it happen!"

"Wonders never cease!" Nick said, returning to the table where two other men sat with a deck of cards. He placed a bottle of whisky on the table and sat down. "Looks like we'll have to find ourselves a different gambling partner," he said pouring drinks all around.

"Archie always shows up here on Sunday night right

after church," a short, stocky man named Toni replied. "Let's get started. He'll be here before the second game, I'll bet you 50 cents he'll be here before the hour's up." Toni slapped a silver coin onto the table.

"I'll take you up on that," Nick said, pulling out his own half dollar. He flipped it into the air and laid it beside Toni's.

Toni lost his 50 cents. The men stayed until the saloon closed but Archie did not appear.

"He'll be here next week," Toni insisted. "I know Archie. He's just like his old man, a drinker and a gambler. It's in his blood. He won't be able to stay away for long."

But Archie wasn't in the saloon the next week nor the week after that. The blood that ran through his veins had been cleansed by the blood of the Lamb. The excitement he had felt when drinking was nothing compared to the exhilaration he felt now. The whole world was new and exciting. He was riding high, enjoying life as he never had before. The desire for alcohol was completely gone. In its place was a consuming passion to follow Jesus. He was determined to be baptized as a public testimony of his adoption into the family of God. The date was already set. It would be the last Sunday in June.

Such a momentous occasion was a time for family rejoicing. His father was too far away to come, but surely Roman would share the happiness with him. There had been many good times together since Roman had come over from the old country four years before. Now he was married to Annie, a lovely girl who had been attending the Baptist church lately. It would make the day perfect to have both of them there for his baptism. The next Sunday after lunch Archie walked over to his brother's place to make his request.

"I'm going to be baptized the last Sunday in June

down at the river. It's a big day in my life. I want you and Annie to be there. Will you come?"

"Attend your baptism? You bet I will . . . with a shot gun!" Roman's eyes were flashing as he pointed his finger at his older brother.

"You . . . you'd kill me, your own brother?" Archie stepped back, for he could see that his brother meant to do just that. "But why?"

"Because you are turning your back on the old ways. You are disgracing our family. Mamma used to say she'd rather see us all dead than become Baptists, turning our backs on all the saints. 'Mary, Mother of Jesus, deliver us from such heresy,' she used to say. How do you think Mamma would feel to see you join with these heretics? How can you shame her so?"

"What shame is it to live a good life? Would you rather I drank and gambled as before?"

"You were baptized already when you were a baby," Roman said. "You don't need to be baptized again."

"That wasn't baptism," Archie explained. "The priest simply sprinkled some water on my head. Jesus went down into the water. I want to follow in His footsteps."

"You will burn in hell for such heresy," Roman continued. "It's better I kill you and save your soul and the souls of my family. Even Annie has been friendly with the Baptists lately. She must see where such a course leads. I hear you don't even pray to the saints any more." Roman's voice rose, "Not even to the blessed Virgin Mary."

"That's right," Archie answered, surprised at his boldness in the face of his brother's anger. "There is only one Mediator between God and man, and that is the Lord Jesus Christ. When I cried out to Him in the barn that night, He heard my prayer and saved me. He has delivered me from the power of the bottle. I didn't need the saints then, nor will I ever need them. Jesus is my Lord and Saviour. He's all I need. I will be baptized the last Sunday of June."

"Try it and see what happens!" Roman threatened. "No brother of mine will be baptized."

Unaware of the threats of her husband, Annie decided to step forward with Archie in giving her life fully over to Jesus. She, too, planned to be baptized the last Sunday in June.

A large crowd gathered on the banks of the North Saskatchewan River that beautiful Sunday. Many came to sing praises to God:

> Blessed assurance, Jesus is mine,
> Oh, what a foretaste of glory divine,
> Heir of salvation, purchase of God,
> Born of His Spirit, washed in His blood.

Others came to laugh at those who were foolish enough to take a bath in the cold waters of the river. Some, like Roman, were intent on putting a stop to the whole affair. But as Roman saw Annie step forward to join Archie in baptism, his fire was gone. It was too late; Annie had made her decision. Probably he should kill them both, but he couldn't, not his own beautiful wife. He loved her too much. Perhaps afterwards he could convince her and his brother of the evil of their ways. Roman watched as Annie and Archie walked down into the water. He listened as Pastor Nisdoly raised his hand towards heaven and said in a loud voice that echoed against the river banks, "I now baptize you in the name of the Father, Son, and Holy Ghost."

Roman watched as Annie came up out of the water, her face radiant, as though she had seen an angel. The same glow was on his brother's face. The joy was reflected on the faces of the other believers singing fervently:

> What a friend we have in Jesus,
> All our sins and griefs to bear,
> What a privilege to carry,
> Everything to God in prayer.

Archie's eyes met those of his brother, who stood sullenly at the edge of the crowd. Roman looked down, unable to understand the look of complete joy and peace on Archie's face. He was ashamed that he could not carry out his threat.

Oh, God, help Roman to find you just as Annie and I have, Archie prayed silently as he took the blanket from the outstretched hands of a deacon at the water's edge.

The June sun warming Archie's body was like a benediction straight from heaven. It was almost as if he could hear his heavenly Father say, "Well done, Archie. You are My son, now. I am pleased with what you did today."

Stupid Sabotnic

The spring of 1920 came to Saskatchewan with the suddenness of a meadow lark's song. Overnight the sky exchanged its winter tang for softness. The snow melted first from the steaming fallow fields, then from the stubble stretches, and finally to uneven patches lying in the ditches along the muddy roads.

Archie's heart sang with the meadowlarks that were on the strawstacks, telephone wires, and fence posts. There was something about the sudden emergence of beauty that made him think of his own rebirth two years before. Archie looked up at the azure blue sky and breathed deeply, inhaling the sweetness of the spring air. The loveliness of the scene made his heart beat faster and his steps quicken.

Crows called to one another from the treetops along the ravines. Farmers, impatient as though this were the only spring left in the world, walked out to their implements, looked them over and planned the seeding. Archie was impatient, too, for spring was the time to look for work and he needed a job.

"You've been a good worker," Mr. Abraham had said, "but my children can help me now. I won't need you any longer."

Archie hadn't minded, because it was spring. Pussy

willows and crocuses bloomed. Green blades of grass pushed through the warming soil. Geese flew overhead at night, their wavering vees pointing north, their far-off calls drifting down. It was time for Archie to move on, too. His old brown suitcase in hand, he walked from farm to farm along the Saskatchewan River. He stopped at last at the farm where his brother Roman was working.

"Try Beaver Creek," Roman suggested. "There's a settlement of Russian Mennonites over there. Perhaps you can get work with them. Go up the river to the ferry. Beaver Creek isn't far on the other side."

"That sounds good to me," said Archie. He set out whistling, giving competition to the meadowlarks. He was still whistling when he walked up the lane to the Naisapayko farm, where he found the farmer in the barnyard, cleaning machinery.

"Do you need a hired hand?" Archie asked. "I'm good with a team of horses."

"You bet I do," said Mr. Naisapayko. "Ready to start today?"

Archie set down his suitcase and began at once to help clean and oil the plow, harrow, and other implements needed for spring planting.

All went well until Saturday morning. After a breakfast of hash-browned potatoes, fried eggs, thick slices of bread freshly baked the day before, and Saskatoon berry jam, Archie pushed back his chair and went to where his jacket hung on a peg beside the door.

"Shall I finish plowing the north quarter?" Archie asked.

"No, don't go to the field today."

"I'll clean the barn, then," Archie suggested. "Then I'll fix that broken harness."

"No, don't clean the barn. Just feed the cattle. You can fix the harness another day. In fact, you can have today off," offered Mr. Naisapayko, settling himself in a rocker by the kitchen stove, an open Bible on his lap.

"Off?" Archie was not sure he had heard correctly. "I don't need off today. Tomorrow is the day I was planning to take off. Tomorrow is Sunday, you know."

"Then take off two days," Mr. Naisapayko smiled and waved his hand to dismiss the matter.

"But, sir, I don't understand," said Archie. "I don't want two days off. Why aren't we working today?"

"Today is the Sabbath."

Archie stood with one hand on the doorknob and stared first at Mr. Naisapayko and then at his wife, who was clearing the table. "What did you say?"

"I said, today is the Sabbath."

"Are you a Jew?"

"No, I'm a Christian. My Bible tells me the seventh day is the Sabbath. God expects everyone to keep it, not just the Jews. Jesus kept the Sabbath when He was on earth, you know."

"Sir, I can't agree with you. Why, everybody keeps Sunday! That's the Lord's Day. That's the day of our Lord's resurrection."

"Sit down, Archie." Mr. Naisapayko motioned to a chair by the table. "I can show you what the Bible says about that."

"No, thank you. I'm not interested," Archie shook his head. "I don't want to work here. I'll find a job where I can work six days a week. I'm not lazy, and I'm not a Jew." Archie took his hand off the doorknob and walked back across the kitchen toward his bedroom. "I'll pack my suitcase."

"I wish you'd stay," Mr. Naisapayko called after him. "You're a fine worker."

"There's no way I'll stay here," Archie mumbled under his breath as he packed his few belongings in the old brown case.

In a short time Archie was on his way. Down the road about a mile was the next farm, owned by a Mennonite family.

"I'd be glad to hire you," Mr. Koronko said. "I don't blame you for not wanting to work for that *Sabotnik* (Sabbathkeeper). You were wise not to listen to his nonsense about the Sabbath. That law was done away with at the cross. I'll tell him that, too, the next time I see him!"

Archie secretly hoped the confrontation would be soon. It would be fun to see his new boss set that stupid Sabotnik straight. However, they didn't see their neighbor over the weekend and Mr. Koronko didn't bring the subject up again. After breakfast on Monday morning Mr. Koronko announced, "Today we'll hitch up two teams of horses, four horses to a team. I'll go ahead to make the guiding furrows and Archie, you'll do the plowing. Can you handle four horses?"

"Sure can." Archie grinned as he tapped his left foot, remembering the day he'd nearly lost it trying to plow with a four-horse team back in Podolsk. A lot of water had gone under the bridge since the accident 10 years before.

Babushka , who had so tenderly wrapped that foot, was dead. His mother had also died during the great war. Archie winced as he thought of his unfulfilled promises to make his mother happy. Now, it was too late.

His father, his brothers, and he had come to Canada before the war. They had missed the horrors of thousands of Russian soldiers who had died for lack of proper food, clothing, and ammunition. There had been a great revolution in his homeland. Ivan was no longer the landlord in Podolsk village. Archie wondered if he had been killed as so many aristocrats had been after the czar's murder. Were the landlord's wife and children in exile in Siberia? Who lived in the beautiful house on the knoll? What about Mary and Zenya? Were they okay? There was so much he longed to know, but communication had been scant because of the war and the revolution.

"Archie!" Mr. Koronko's voice brought him back to Canada and the present. Today he would plow with a team of four horses in Koronko's field. "Archie, are you all right?"

"Oh, I'm fine." Archie finished his coffee and stood. "I was just thinking about all the times I've plowed with four horses. Ivan, the landlord, had a team like this back in the old country."

"Not any more," Mr. Koronko commented. "Not if what the papers say is true. The landlords finally got what was coming to them. We'd better get busy. I'd like to finish that south quarter today." The two men dressed and went silently to the barn to harness the horses. Each was thinking of the old country and loved ones separated by thousands of miles of prairies, mountains, water, and a world at war.

"An apple doesn't fall far from the apple tree." His mother's words came back to him as clearly as if she had said them at the breakfast table that morning. Funny they should come back to him now.

"For once you were wrong, Mamma," Archie whispered into the horse's ear as he adjusted the harness. Archie looked up at the sky and wondered if she could hear him. Surely, if she was in heaven as the preacher had said, then she must be looking down, now watching him harness horses. She must realize how far he had come. Yes, how very far he had traveled, physically from his home in Podolsk and spiritually from his Russian Orthodox upbringing. It's true he had started out to be very much like his father, a drinker and a gambler, but God had reached down and picked up this rotten apple of a man and given him new life in Christ Jesus.

"Ho!" Archie shouted to his team as he slapped the flank of the right lead horse. "We've got a job to do today. Let's get moving."

Carefully, Archie guided the plow along the guide furrows Mr. Koronko had made. Looking back over his shoulder he was proud of the neat rows of rich brown earth he was making. There were no hard paths to cross on this farm. The steel blades cut sharply into the soil, turning great lumps of fresh earth, placing the stubble of last year's crop deep under the ground where it could provide nourishment for this year's grain.

Looking forward again, Archie saw Mr. Koronko pulling on the reins, slowing his team for a turn at the pile of stones that marked the boundary line between his and Mr. Naisapayko's property.

Mr. Naisapayko was approaching the same spot from the opposite direction. He waved and shouted, "*Dobray ranuk* (Good morning)!"

Mr. Koronko stopped his team and waited for his neighbor to arrive. Archie couldn't hear what his boss said, but he noticed Mr. Naisapayko stop his team and walk over to where the other man stood, feet spread, hands on hips, holding the reins of his horses. As Archie's team drew close, Mr. Koronko turned and waved his arm in a wide arc, pointing back towards the house. Archie turned his team and plowed without the guiding furrow, for his boss continued talking.

Back and forth across the field Archie plowed, conscious of the fine job he was doing alone but curious as to what the two neighbors were discussing. At one point Archie noticed Mr. Koronko pound his right fist into his left palm and he knew they must be arguing and his boss was not going to give in.

The sun was nearly overhead before Mr. Koronko caught up with Archie halfway down the field.

"What happened?" Archie asked.

"Stupid Sabotnik!" Mr. Koronko spat on the ground to show his disgust. "He doesn't know anything. I tried to tell him that Christians should keep Sunday in honor of the resurrection but he kept quoting the Fourth Commandment."

"The commandments were for the Jews," Archie said.

"Exactly!" Mr. Koronko agreed. "I told him the law was nailed to the cross."

"What did he say to that?"

"Christ came to fulfill the law, not to destroy it. I never heard of such a thing. Then I tried to tell him the apostles kept Sunday and he denied it. He said that Christians kept Saturday until 323 A.D. when Constantine, emperor of Rome, made a decree to worship on Sunday."

"Nonsense!" said Archie. "If that was so, why wouldn't the preachers know about it. They're a lot better educated than Naisapayko. He's lucky to have had eight years of schooling at the most."

"I know that, but I couldn't convince him. He's bull-headed. Stubborn as a mule! Won't listen."

"I'll bet Reverend Nisdoly could make him see the light," suggested Archie. "He's really smart and a powerful preacher. People say even the devil is scared to come to his church for fear he might get converted!"

"Hmmph!" grunted Mr. Koronko, starting up his team again. "Somebody needs to straighten Naisapayko out before he upsets the peace of the whole community with his weird ideas."

Sabbath Debate

Talk about the new religion grew faster than the young shoots of grain. By harvest time interest in the Sabbath question had ripened into a real problem for the community of Beaver Creek.

"Something has got to be done," Mr. Koronko declared as he slammed his fist down on the counter in the feed store. A group of farmers had spent the better part of the morning hashing over all they knew about the Sabotniks.

"Those Seventh-day Adventists think they are so smart, quoting Scripture and getting us all mixed up!" Mr. Koronko continued. "I think it's time we found somebody to set them straight. If we don't do something they'll spread their falsehoods throughout the community."

"Hear! Hear!" agreed a Baptist farmer. "I suggest a public debate in the Baptist church, since that's the biggest place available. Let the Adventists send one of their preachers to debate the question with one of our preachers."

"I'm sure Reverend Nisdoly could beat their best," suggested Archie. "He really knows his Bible!"

So it was that Elder Babienko of the Adventists was scheduled to debate the Sabbath question with Pastor

Nisdoly of the Baptists one Friday evening. A third man, a Mennonite, was to be the timekeeper. Each man would get 20 minutes to give his beliefs and the other preacher would have a chance at rebuttal.

"Since Mr. Babienko is our guest tonight, we will give him first chance to express his opinions on the topic of the Sabbath versus Sunday as the Lord's Day," Pastor Nisdoly said, bowing graciously to his debater on the platform.

"Thank you, Pastor," Elder Babienko began. "I am honored to be called here tonight to discuss this vital topic. The Sabbath—is it Saturday or Sunday? The answer is much too important to depend on any man's ideas. I have not come here to give you my opinion but to share with you what God's Word has to say on this important subject. Turn with me please to the second chapter of Genesis, where we find the first mention of the Sabbath.

"In the Garden of Eden, before there was a Christian or a Jew, God gave the Sabbath to man as a memorial of His creation. When He gave the Ten Commandments on Mount Sinai the Sabbath was already in existence. For 40 years in the wilderness, God worked a miracle every week by giving a double portion of manna on the sixth day so that the people need not gather manna on the Sabbath. When God wrote the fourth commandment with His own finger, as you read it in Exodus 20, notice that He said, 'Remember.'

"Notice also that the commandment says, 'the seventh day.' I ask you, what day is that? Look on your calendars. Which day is the seventh day? Saturday, of course. Any school boy knows that!

"If there is still any question about which day the Lord has commanded us to keep holy, turn with me to Luke 23 and begin reading at verse 54. It says here they prepared spices and rested the Sabbath day according to the commandment. Now, I ask you, which day was that? The first verse of the next chapter says, 'Upon the first day of the week, very early in the morning, they came unto the sepulcher, bringing the spices which they had prepared.' Now, on which day did our Lord rise from the dead? On which day did the women come to the tomb to anoint his body? Here we definitely have the Sabbath fixed as the Saturday between Good Friday and Easter Sunday.''

There was a murmur of voices throughout the sanctuary as he took his seat and the Baptist minister stood.

''I am willing to concede your point that the Sabbath of the Fourth Commandment is Saturday. However, we do not keep the Sabbath of the Old Testament any longer. We are now operating under a new and better covenant. We Christians observe Sunday in honor of the resurrection of our Lord and Savior, for it was, as Pastor Babienko brought out, upon the first day of the week that our Lord rose from the grave.''

''The apostles met together on the first day of the week in the upper room following the resurrection. There are several instances mentioned where the apostles met together on Sunday and we have been doing it ever since. I ask you, Mr. Babienko, how it is that the apostles were gathered together on Sunday if it was not to honor the day of our Lord's resurrection?''

People sat on the edge of their seats. A hush fell over the entire assembly as the Adventist minister deftly flicked the pages of his Bible, then stood to answer the question.

''If you will open your Bibles to John 20:19 you will find why the disciples were gathered together. It was not to worship. John says it was 'for fear of the Jews.'

''Now turn with me to Acts 20:7-11 for the answer to your second question. This is the only case in the entire book of Acts where there is a record of a Sunday meeting. This was an evening service, probably Saturday evening. It was obviously a special meeting that continued all night, inasmuch as Paul was planning to depart the next day.

"Actually, contrary to what our brother has just said, the Book of Acts reveals that the only day on which the apostles repeatedly were engaged in worship services on a weekly basis was on Saturday, the seventh day of the week. Notice Acts 13:14 and 44, Acts 16:13, and Acts 17:2. Acts 18 tells us that Paul worshipped on Sabbath for a year and a half while he was in Corinth.

"It is clear to me that the apostles followed in the footsteps of their Lord in worshiping every Sabbath as we read in Luke 4:16, 'As his custom was he went into the synagogue on the Sabbath day and stood up for to read.'"

Heads began to nod in agreement around the room. One woman stood and said, "Let's stop this debate. The more this man talks the more he will have everyone believing his way. We don't want to listen to his falsehoods any longer."

"No! I want to hear what he has to say," protested another woman, jumping to her feet in protest. "We will hear the debate to the end because we want to find out the truth."

The debate continued. Elder Babienko answered the objections one by one with a verse of Scripture.

"The law was done away with at the cross," insisted Pastor Nisdoly.

"Not so," came back Elder Babienko. "The Ten Commandment law of God is eternal. There is nothing wrong with it. Read Psalm 19:7, where David says, 'The law of the Lord is perfect.' The apostle Paul said, 'Wherefore the law is holy, and the commandment holy, and just, and good.' Jesus himself said that He came not to destroy the law and the prophets, but to fulfill them. See Matthew 5:17. It was Jesus Himself who said, 'If ye love me, keep my commandments'—John 14:15.''

After three hours of debate, Elder Babienko closed his Bible and stepped to the edge of the platform. Extending his arms toward the audience he said, ''How many of you have had your eyes opened tonight about the truth of the Sabbath as found in God's Word? Who now believes that the Ten Commandment law of God is still binding today? Who wants to step out into the light of truth and follow Jesus in keeping holy the seventh day of the week as He has commanded?''

Archie jumped to his feet, followed by Mr. Koronko. Twenty-four others joined them. The meeting broke up in confusion as everyone began to talk at once about what they had heard.

Mr. Naisapayko pushed through the crowd to the side of Archie and Mr. Koronko. ''The Lord be praised!'' he exclaimed, giving each a warm bear hug.

''I hate to admit it, but you were right that day in the field,'' Koronko said.

''Winning the argument doesn't matter,'' Mr. Naisapayko stated. ''The important thing is that you now see the light!''

''That we do,'' agreed Archie. ''How could we help but see it after the way Pastor Babienko explained it tonight. I never knew all those things were in the Bible.''

''Come join us for worship tomorrow,'' Mr. Naisapayko invited. ''We'd love to have you.''

''Well, maybe sometime,'' said Mr. Koronko as he and Archie headed for the door. ''I've other plans for tomorrow.''

What those plans were Archie didn't discover until the following morning.

The smell of frying onions crept under the bedroom

door and awoke Archie with a start. Had he slept so late? Usually he was up and had the horses fed before breakfast. The first rays of sunlight caught in the icy frost crystals on his windowpane and splintered into a thousand diamonds across the glass.

Archie blinked at the brightness, yawned, and snuggled deeper under the downy comforter. Today was Saturday, the Sabbath, as Elder Babienko had so clearly explained last night. He had pledged to keep it holy. He could begin by getting his extra 40 winks that was his usual due on Sunday mornings. It was a good feeling to have the Sabbath question settled at last in his own mind. He sensed within himself the same calmness he had noticed Mr. Naisapayko have that Saturday morning in the spring when Archie had been angry at the thought of taking Saturday off. Now he relished the idea because he knew it was right. The blessing of the Sabbath that Pastor Babienko had said God had placed in this day at Creation seemed to wrap itself around him like a blanket and make him feel at peace with himself and the world.

"Archie!" Mr. Koronko's voice didn't sound very peaceful. In fact, he sounded a bit agitated. "Archie! It's time to get up!"

"Okay, I'm coming," Archie threw back the covers and shivered in the crisp air of his unheated bedroom. The clothes he had worn to the meeting last night were on the chair beside his bed. He put them on as quickly as he could and went out to join the Koronkos for breakfast. He noticed that Mr. Koronko had already eaten and was pulling on his boots at the back door. He had on overalls and a parka.

"*Dobray ranuk,*" Archie greeted Mr. and Mrs. Koronko as he sat down at his place for breakfast. Mrs. Koronko piled his plate with verenykye and poured him a cup of coffee. Mr. Koronko finished lacing his boots, then he pulled some papers off a wire hook that hung on the kitchen wall.

"I'd say it's about time you got up!" Mr. Koronko scolded. "We've got those two loads of wheat to get in to Purdue this morning. I've fed and harnessed the horses for you. We'll go as soon as you finish your breakfast. Make it snappy!"

"But surely you don't plan to take the grain today?"

"Why not? We loaded the wagons yesterday with that in mind. You know that!"

"Yes, but didn't you stand last night saying you were going to keep the seventh-day Sabbath?"

"Of course, and I intend to keep the Sabbath after today. First we've got to get this grain to Purdue."

"Don't you think we've trampled enough Sabbaths when we were ignorant? Why should we do it now that we know what is right?"

Mr. Koronko rubbed his forehead as if to erase the knowledge gained last night from his mind. At last he took off his parka and straddled the chair opposite Archie. "You're right, of course. But what shall we do about the wheat?"

"We could cover it so the horses and cattle can't get into it."

"True. I've got those canvas squares we used at harvest. I guess if we tied them down securely the wheat would be safe enough."

"We can take the grain to Purdue on Monday morning," Archie added. "I'm sure it won't spoil by then."

"We'll just have to trust the Lord to take care of it for us over the weekend. Surely if He cared for us all these years when we've been keeping the wrong day, He'll take care of us when we are doing what's right."

"Of course He will," Archie agreed.

"Do you suppose there's time to get ready for church? It shouldn't take us too long to cover the wagons and hitch up a team to the old democrat. What about it, Mother?" Mr. Koronko smiled at his wife who was scraping dishes into the bucket for the pigs.

"I'll be ready by the time you are," she said.

"Well, looks like that's settled." Mr. Koronko got up and headed for the door. "Come on, Archie, let's get those wagons covered. "

"I'll unhitch the horses while you get the canvas," Archie replied.

Archie led two of the horses back to their stalls in the warm barn. He led the other team to the carriage parked in the lean-to beside the tool shed. By the time he had the horses hitched to the carriage his boss was calling from the barnyard.

"Come, Archie. I need your help to fasten these ropes down securely."

By nine o'clock they were on their way to the little white Adventist church in Beaver Creek. Mr. and Mrs. Koronko, dressed in their Sunday best, were seated in the carriage while Archie drove the team for their first time to an Adventist meeting.

The familiar strains of "Nearer My God to Thee" were rolling out of the little pump organ when they drove into the churchyard. They were not the first ones there, by any means. Wagons and carriages of every description filled the large grassy area near the church. Horses, tied to their posts, were quietly munching the hay left for them by their owners.

Mr. Naisapayko was at the door to greet them. "Welcome, neighbors!" he exclaimed, extending his hand to Mr. Koronko. "We were praying you'd come this morning."

Mr. Koronko winked at Archie. "Looks like the Lord answered your prayer, 'cause I sure wasn't planning to come."

"We hope you'll come every week," Mr. Naisapayko

said as he ushered them into the already crowded church.

The only spot available was in the second row from the front. They squeezed into the bench to sit by the side of a plump Russian grandmother wearing a blue kerchief. Her wrinkled face broke into a wide toothless smile. Suddenly self-conscious, she covered her mouth with her right hand. The gesture made Archie think of Babushka. How often he had seen her do that very thing. How he missed her! How he wished he could tell her about the marvelous change in his life . . . his conversion . . . his baptism . . . and now his discovery of the wonderful Sabbath truth.

Archie's eyes blurred as he thought of long-ago evenings sitting around Babushka's table, and of his loved ones now dead. It was too late to share with them, but there was still his father. *I will go to him this Christmas*, Archie decided. *That would be the perfect time to tell him the good news about what God has done in my life.*

Christmas Courage

rchie poured a cup of sour cream into the pot of borscht simmering on the back of his father's old iron cookstove, and stirred the soup. The thick cream made white swirls in the red broth. Like a Christmas candy cane, he thought. He covered the soup and turned his attention to the herring frying in the crusty black skillet on front of the stove. He turned the fish and smiled at its golden crispness.

Every time he smelled fish frying Archie thought of Mamma cooking the fish he had caught in the river behind Podolsk village. These tonight would taste nothing like Mamma's herring in tomato sauce or her stuffed pike; but at least it was fish, and he would share it with Papa and Roman for the traditional Christmas Eve celebration.

Before going to her folks for Christmas, Annie had made kolach, the round braided Christmas bread, and it sat now in the center of Samuel Shipowick's wooden table. Beside it were plates of poppy seed rolls and *medivnyk* (honey cake) that they had brought with them from Beaver Creek.

Samuel Shipowick stood now at the front window watching Roman shovel a narrow path through the four feet of snow to the road. Archie wondered if his father were thinking of Mamma and Podolsk too. He had retreated inward since he had learned of Domka's death. It was as if all his hard work were now for nothing. It seemed to Archie that his father had aged 20 years in the last two. The spring was gone from his step and the laughter from his heart. Archie went now to stand by his father and put an arm around his drooping shoulders.

"Look, Papa," Archie said, pointing to a lone star that shimmered in the gray sky above the frozen prairie. "The star is out; it's time to eat our Christmas supper."

"So it is," Samuel agreed. He took a deep breath and exhaled slowly, as if to rid himself of the deep melancholy that was building in his soul. "Call Roman."

Archie opened the door of the cabin and called, "Come and get it! Supper's on!"

Roman stamped his feet on the path as he walked toward the open door. Once inside he swept off his boots with the broom that was kept propped beside the door. He shook the snow off his parka and hung it on a hook beside his father's. "Smells good," he said.

Archie dished up the food while the two other men sat down opposite each other at the table.

"Sit down, Archie," Samuel Shipowick said with a bit of the old agitation Archie remembered from his teenage years. What had he done now? Probably nothing more than make him think of the old country.

Archie looked with pity at the lonely man and thought, *I wish I could share my happiness with you. The joy I've had since I found the Lord is something you need. I hope to share the Sabbath truth with you, too, while I am here.*

On the journey from Beaver Creek to Meath Park, Archie had been able to share with Roman a little of the new truths he had been learning. He longed to see his family accept the Adventist message, but now wasn't the time. Maybe tonight after a good meal his father would be in the mood to talk. "Well, Papa," Archie stopped his reverie long enough to ask, "will you say the blessing?"

The three bowed their heads as Samuel Shipowick mumbled the ancient Slavic blessing Archie had heard so many times as a child. It brought tears to his eyes as he remembered his family as it used to be. How he missed Mamma and Babushka!

"I wonder what Mary and Zenya are doing tonight?" Roman voiced all their thoughts.

"I hope they are all well," Archie said.

"Remember the last time we were together as a family for Christmas?" Roman reminisced.

"Yes," Archie brightened. "I was 13 and you were 11."

"You're right," Roman agreed. "That was the last Christmas before you left home to stay with Babushka."

Samuel Shipowick pulled out a big red handkerchief from his pocket and blew his nose. Archie and Roman exchanged knowing glances.

"How was your wheat crop this year?" Archie changed the subject.

"Fair to middling," Samuel replied. "Enough to get by."

A smile crossed Samuel's face then. He pushed his plate away and stood. "Just remembered something," he said, disappearing into the bedroom. He came out with an unopened bottle of vodka in his hand.

"I bought it when I heard you were coming," he grinned. "I've saved it all this time." He set the bottle beside the kolach and went to the small cupboard where he kept his dishes. He brought back three glasses and set them on the table. He uncorked the bottle and poured out a half glass for each of his boys and one for himself. He pushed a glass across the table towards Roman and Archie. "It's Christmas," he said. "Let's have a drink for the old country."

Archie swallowed twice, then cleared his throat.

"Come on, boys, drink," Samuel Shipowick demanded as he lifted his own glass and waited for them to follow suit.

"I don't drink this stuff any more," Archie said, looking straight into his father's steel blue eyes.

Samuel Shipowick set down his glass. Resting both hands on the table, he leaned towards Archie as if a closer look would help him make sense of what was happening. He had offered a glass of liquor to his sons, as was the custom for Russian fathers to do on Christmas Eve. Archie had actually refused. Archie, who was a bigger drinker than he himself had ever thought of being. "Archie, are you sick?" he said at last.

"No, I'm not sick, but . . ." Archie groped for words to explain tactfully how God had picked him up and turned him around. That experience in the hayloft had led him to give up drinking. The path of obedience to his Savior that he had started walking that awful night had led him to baptism into the Baptist Church and eventually into the Seventh-day Adventist Church.

Before Archie could think of how to begin, Roman spoke up. "Archie has become a Sabotnik," he said.

"What?"

"Archie has become a Sabotnik," Roman repeated.

"Is that true?" Samuel bellowed. His face contorted. His neck grew red.

"Yes, sir, it is true," Archie replied.

"So, you think you're now better than the rest of us," Samuel spat out the words. "Can't even have a drink with your old Papa. Too good, you are!" He pounded the table, making the dishes rattle.

Archie stood and circled the table to try to reason

with his dad, to calm him somehow. Such anger could cause a heart attack at his father's age.

"Get away from me," Samuel Shipowick snarled. He stepped back as his eldest son reached out towards him. "You have disgraced me and your blessed mother. Sabotnik! Bah!" He strode to the back door and went out onto the porch. In a moment he returned, axe raised above his head. He lunged at Archie. "You're no son of mine!" he stormed.

"No, Papa!" Roman screamed and Archie ducked. As Roman grabbed his father's arms they went limp by his side. The axe dropped to the floor.

"Get out of here! Both of you," Samuel ordered. He pointed to the door with a trembling hand. "I don't want to look at your faces. Be gone!"

Hurriedly Roman and Archie put on their boots and parkas. They wrapped their woolen scarves around their chins and walked out into the starlit night, leaving Samuel still standing in the middle of the kitchen with the axe at his feet.

* * *

The tinting green and mauve of the Northern Lights rippled across the prairie sky. Like someone waving a giant flag, the colors danced and faded only to reappear in another place. It was as though they were blown across the sky by a phantom wind. Its ghostly song could be heard in the tops of the poplars. Its icy fingers reached down to sweep the snow smooth and pile it in ridges against the fences. It pulled at Archie's and Roman's parkas, causing them to draw their coats tighter about them.

The two brothers stood facing each other at the place where the lane reached the road.

"What shall we do?" Roman asked. "It's a long way to Prince Albert."

"Twenty-five miles," replied Archie. "We'll never make it in this wind."

"Not if we have to walk, and I can't imagine anyone going by sled at this time of night."

"Let's go to Kovich's," Archie suggested.

"Good idea," Roman nodded. "They'll not turn us out." The young men began a brisk walk towards the nearest farm, two and a half miles down the road.

The night was still except for the sighing of the wind and the crunch of fresh snow under their boots. For several minutes they walked in silence, each wrapped in his own thoughts of the encounter with their dad. From somewhere to the left a coyote howled and the wind blew back a reply from the right.

"I did it again!" Archie said at last. "I seem to have the knack of making Papa mad." He shuddered as he remembered the wild look in his father's eyes as he came at him with the axe.

"He meant to kill you," Roman said.

"I know it. Thanks for your help."

"Now he's mad at both of us. You should have drunk a little, just to please him."

"It was a real struggle," Archie admitted. "I wanted so much to make Papa happy, but I just couldn't take that drink."

"Why not?" Roman asked. "That's what insulted him. After all, he is your father and you know he expects to be obeyed. You were taught that as well as I. You've gotten into trouble every time you've crossed him, so why did you do it tonight?"

"Then I would have been hurting my heavenly Father," explained Archie softly. "I had to choose. I couldn't please both."

"I thought the Bible says to honor your father and mother. Wouldn't you have been honoring Papa by taking a little of the drink he had saved for us?'' Roman was puzzled.

''The Bible also says that we ought to obey God rather than man. I made a vow to the Lord that night in the hayloft and I intend to keep it. If I am to be a Christian, I have no other choice.''

''You really take this religion business seriously, don't you? Who would have thought this is the way things would turn out?''

''I'm sorry I've spoiled your Christmas.''

''I wasn't thinking of tonight. . . I was thinking of the night after Papa left for Canada . . . you know, the night you danced in his place?''

''That was some night! Everybody said how much I looked like Papa . . . acted like him . . . drank like him. After that night I came to believe I had no other choice but to be like him. Remember what Mamma used to say, 'An apple doesn't fall far from the apple tree'?''

''You've sure proved her wrong! You're a long ways from being like Papa.''

''Oh, I don't know that I've proved anything.'' Archie shook his head and sighed. ''I remember how hard I tried not to be like Papa, but the harder I tried the more like him I got. Any change is not my doing. I can only thank the Lord for what He has done.''

''All that Bible readin' and goin' to meetin' is makin' you sound like a preacher! I feel a sermon comin' on!'' Roman laughed. ''But how about saving it for another day. I see the lights. Let's make a run for it!''

Archie said no more but settled into a steady rhythm beside his brother. He wasn't ready to tell anyone yet that to be a preacher was exactly what he was thinking. He wanted to make sure of God's plan for his life before he shared it with anyone.

The sound of a Russian carol drifted out to them across the snow. Through the window they saw Mr.

Kovich seated on a chair beside an open fire, playing the accordion. His boys sat on the bench opposite him, swaying in time to the music. Mrs. Kovich was clearing the table. Roman knocked. The music stopped and the door swung open.

"Merry Christmas. Christ is born!" Archie said.

"Let us adore Him" was the reply. The Kovich boys stood beside their father. "Come in. Come in," Mr. Kovich invited, pulling the half-frozen youths into the warm room.

"What a pleasant surprise!" exclaimed Mrs. Kovich. "Come have a cup of poor man's coffee. I roasted it myself from this year's wheat and barley."

Archie and Roman pulled a bench up to the table still spread with kolach, Christmas cake, cookies, and rolls. The hot liquid felt good after their walk in the cold.

"You should have brought Samuel with you," Mr. Kovich said. "We'd love to see him."

"Papa ordered us out of the house," Archie explained. "It's too far to walk to Prince Albert tonight. We thought maybe we could sleep here."

"Of course, of course," said Mr. Kovich. "But why did he order you out? I can't believe that of Samuel."

"He offered us the traditional liquor after supper," Roman replied. "Archie refused to drink with Papa."

"I couldn't," Archie explained. "It isn't that I wanted to show disrespect for Papa, but I made a vow to the Lord that I wouldn't drink any more. I couldn't break that vow."

"You poor boys," Mrs. Kovich sympathized as she refilled their cups. "Help yourself to bread and cake while I fix a bed for you."

"We'd be glad for a place on the floor by your fire," Roman said.

"Nothing doing." Mrs. Kovich was already pulling a straw tick out from under their own bed. "This will be a lot better. I've got plenty of warm comforters."

"Samuel must have been drinking," Mr. Kovich commented after listening to the whole story of Mr. Shipowick and the axe. "He wouldn't do that if he were sober, even if he were insulted. Sleep here tonight and go back tomorrow. I'm sure he'll be over it by then."

"You don't know Papa as well as we do," Archie said, remembering his troubled teenage years. "He'll need longer than that to cool down. We'll go on to Prince Albert tomorrow where we can catch a train to Borden."

The bed made up, Mrs. Kovich joined the men around the fire. "Let's sing some carols," she begged. "That will make us happy before we sleep." They sang until nearly midnight, happy, carefree carols of the old country that Archie remembered singing in Podolsk.

When the lights were out and he could hear the even breathing of his brother beside him, Archie sat up and stared for a long time at the glowing coals of the fire thinking about the events of the evening . . . of his life. At last he reached for his jacket, which lay on the bench beside the fire, and took out his Bible. In the flickering light he read: "Fear thou not; for I am with thee: be not dismayed; for I am thy God: I will strengthen thee; yea, I will help thee; yea, I will uphold thee with the right hand of my righteousness" (Isa. 41:10).

The words lit a fire of warm joy in Archie's heart, melting away the disappointment he had felt at being turned out of his father's house on Christmas Eve.

"Thank you, God, for giving me strength to do the right thing tonight," Archie whispered. "Without You how different my life would be!"

Epilogue

Archie became a literature evangelist to earn money to attend school so that he could become a minister. During the summer he married Laura, the daughter of one of his customers. They helped raise up a new company of believers at Fenwood, Saskatchewan. Archie decided to delay his education for a year in order to help establish the new church. With the birth of their first son, Archie gave up his plans to go back to school and became a full-time farmer.

Archie and Laura raised seven sons. Larry is a dentist, Victor a minister, and Lewis a nursing home manager. Walter, Winston, and Tom chose farming as a career. All are active leaders in their local churches. The seventh son, Elmer, made his decision to follow the Lord just three days before a tragic accident took his life.

Archie's father, Samuel, never did become an Adventist Christian, though he often welcomed Archie and his family to his home.

Archie was an elder of the Fenwood and Yorkton, Saskatchewan, Adventist churches, and a faithful witness to the power of God to change lives, until his death in 1985.